EDITOR: MARTIN WINDROW

OSPREY
MILITARY

MEN-AT-ARMS SERIES · 169

RESISTANCE WARFARE 1940-45

Text by
CARLOS CABALLERO JURADO
Translated by
ANUNCIACION SOMAVILLA
Colour plates by
PAUL HANNON

Published in 1985 by
Osprey Publishing Ltd,
59 Grosvenor Street, London, W1X 9DA
© Copyright 1985 Osprey Publishing Ltd
Reprinted 1986, 1989, 1990, 1992

British Library Cataloguing in Publication Data

Caballero-Jurado, Carlos
  Resistance warfare, 1940–1945.—(Men-at-arms
  series; 169)
  1. World War, 1939–1945—Underground movements
  I. Title   II. Series
  940.53′4   D802.E9

ISBN 0-85045-638-X

Filmset in Great Britain
Printed in Hong Kong

Dedication
This book is dedicated to my mother.

Acknowledgements
The author gratefully acknowledges the invaluable
assistance of the following:
Alfredo Campello, for assistance with picture research;
David Littlejohn, author of *The Patriotic Traitors* and
Foreign Legions of the Third Reich, for his help with the
Italian and French sections; Hans W. Neulen, author
of *Eurofaschismus und der Zweite Weltkrieg* and *An
Deutscher Seite: Internationale Freiwillige von Wehrmacht
und Waffen-SS*, for his help with the Scandinavian,
Dutch and Italian sections; Michelle Rallo, for his
help with the Italian section; Frans Selleslagh of the
Centre de Recherches et d'Etudes de la Seconde
Guerre Mondiale, Brussels; Nigel Thomas, co-author
of *Germany's Eastern Front Allies 1941–45* and *Partisan
Warfare 1941–45* in this series, for his help with the
French and Italian sections; Dr Trumpp of the
Federal German *Bundesarchiv*; and Jan Vincx, author
of *Vlaanderen in Uniform, 1940–45*, for his help with the
Belgian section.

Artist's Note
Readers may care to note that the original paintings
from which the colour plates in this book were
prepared are available for private sale. All
reproduction copyright whatsoever is retained by the
publisher. All enquiries should be addressed to:
  Paul Hannon
  90 Station Road
  Kings Langley
  Herts. WD4 8LB
The publishers regret that they can enter into no
correspondence upon this matter.

Editor's Note
This book deals with Norway, Denmark, Holland,
Belgium, France and Italy. The companion volume
MAA 142 *Partisan Warfare 1941–45*, by Nigel Thomas
and Peter Abbott, covers parallel developments in
Poland, Russia (including the Ukraine, Byelorussia
and the Baltic Republics), Yugoslavia, Albania and
Greece.

Introduction

The occupation of Western Europe by the Wehrmacht brought about the birth of resistance movements in all the countries affected—and also collaborationist movements, directly opposed to the resistance. The war against Germany became a civil war, more or less violent, within each country. During the 1930s, and particularly between 1933 and 1939, Europe had been divided between two political blocs—anti-Fascism, and anti-Communism. These two broad political attitudes naturally evolved during the 1940s into resistance and collaboration movements. For many years since the end of the Second World War the resisters have been presented in a universally heroic light—the collaborators, as criminals. According to this scenario the resistance was a popular movement with patriotic aims, while the collaborators were a group of villainous traitors who sold out to the Germans. Today, this simplistic version of events can hardly be sustained.

There were patriots and opportunists, heroes and criminals in the ranks of both Resistance and Collaboration. For many, the choice was simply between two different views of the destiny of their country. For the anti-Fascists the priority was the destruction of German Fascism, with Allied help. For the anti-Communists, German help was necessary for the destruction of the 'Bolshevik menace', even if the price of German occupation had to be paid.

Italy and France excepted, the resistance movements had little value as a military contribution to the Allied cause in Western Europe. They never represented a serious military danger for the Germans; neither were they of significant assistance to Allied operations on the battlefield. They always needed abundant help from outside. Without the participation of the British SOE, and the arms drops which they could organise, the resistance

NCO of German Police wearing the piped service tunic with an eight-button front, dark brown collar and cuffs, and bright green piping. The wreathed Police version of the national eagle-and-swastika is worn in green on the left arm and in silver on the cap. Note that Police NCOs did not wear the 9 mm silver braid—*Tresse*—round their collars, a peculiarity later extended to some of the foreign auxiliary forces raised under Police sponsorship. (Bundesarchiv)

would in many cases have represented little more than a gesture.

Though resistance began, tentatively, in 1940, the real date of its birth as a significant movement was 1941, coinciding with Hitler's invasion of Soviet Russia. In 1940 European Communist parties had criticised or frankly sabotaged the war effort against Germany in their own countries, in accordance with the Nazi-Soviet Pact; in 1941 they suddenly discovered in themselves a more robust patriotism. In 1939 Maurice Thorez, general secretary of the French Communist Party, deserted from the French Army and fled to Russia, urging his followers to do likewise; he was stripped of his French nationality. In 1941 he ordered his followers to throw themselves into a violent guerrilla campaign against the Germans—to save France; or to help Russia? De Gaulle himself warned the French Communists of the harm their methods brought down upon the French population. They did not take much notice: their attacks, locally successful, provoked indiscriminate German reprisals, which in turn attracted recruits to the Communists' cause. As the early Christians had found under Roman persecution, 'the blood of the martyrs is the seed of the Church'.

The Communists were the only faction within the resistance movements who had previous knowledge of underground political activity and the techniques of revolutionary insurrection. They used their training to infiltrate other resistance organisations, and to manipulate them for the long-term advantage of the Communist cause, looking beyond the eventual liberation of their countries from the Germans. They were the most disciplined and efficient of all the resisters; and consequently their

Customs officials—*Zollbeamten*—played an important part in fighting the logistic organisation of Resistance movements; here, they check a French fishing boat. Uniforms are in field grey, with dark green Waffenfarbe and dark green and silver insignia; the cuff band shows a silver eagle and swastika on a silver-edged green band. Rank is indicated by shoulder straps, collar patches and also cap cords. (Bundesarchiv)

membership increased, even though some wartime recruits did not share their ideology. As the Communists were the hard core of active resistance, collaborationist authorities were able to turn the patriotic argument against them; their propaganda presented resistance movements in general not as patriots, but as Russian agents determined to impose on their countries a Stalinist dictatorship.

German Security Forces

The **Hohere SS und Polizeiführer** or HSSPF ('High Command of the SS and Police') were responsible for security in occupied Western Europe. There were HSSPF in Norway, Denmark, Holland, Belgium and France. In Italy this command was designated Höchster SS und Polizeiführer; held by one of Himmler's favourites, SS Gen. Wolff, it embraced two separate HSSPF— HSSPF 'Oberitalien', and HSSPF 'Adriatisches Kustenland'.

The German security forces in the West were less important than those deployed in the East, for a number of reasons. Firstly, the resistance movements themselves were less important; secondly, Western terrain offered far less space and cover for resistance activities; and thirdly, other means were locally available—in all occupied Western countries the national police forces remained in existence, and in many of them large numbers of Wehrmacht regulars were stationed to ward off Allied invasion.

The first German security forces transferred to the Western countries were several Standarte (regiments) of the **SS-Totenkopfverbände** or SS-TV—'SS Death's-Head Units'. The 14th SS-TV Standarte was established in Denmark, the 6th and 7th in Norway, and the 4th and 11th in Holland. In February 1941 these units were disbanded and their personnel transferred to the Waffen-SS[1]. (The only peculiarity of their uniforms had been the use of the death's-head instead of the SS-runes on the collar patch.)

Very few **Police Regiments** (retitled 'SS-Police Regiments' from 1943) were sent to Western countries on a permanent basis. The Police Regts.

[1]See MAA 34, *The Waffen-SS*, for explanation of the relationship between these different organisations.

Photographed at an inter-unit ski competition in occupied Norway, these Police personnel display useful uniform details. The distinctive style of Police shoulder straps is displayed by the bending figure at the right; and note Police collar patches, which for enlisted men and NCOs bore the silver-grey *Litzen* on Police green backing piped in silver-grey. Officers wore their larger silver *Litzen* on unpiped green backing. Generals—as extreme right—wore Wehrmacht-style gold oakleaf patches on Police green backing until autumn 1942: see under Plate A3. (Bundesarchiv)

'Nordnorwegen' and 'Sudnorwegen' (later retitled 26th and 27th SS-Police Regts.) were established in Norway. They were reinforced by the 7th and 15th Police Regts., the latter subsequently transferred to Italy. In Denmark there were only two Police Guard Battalions, established in 1943; Holland had the 3rd Police Regt.; and in Belgium no German Police deployment was felt necessary. The 4th, 14th, 19th and 29th Police Regts. served in France for short periods; and an *ad hoc* unit, Police Regt. 'Griese', was created to participate in the occupation of the so-called 'Free Zone' of Vichy southern France in November 1942.

The situation in Italy was very different. The 10th, 12th and 15th Police Regts. served in that country; and important police forces were also recruited among ethnic Germans (*Volksdeutsche*) from the Southern Tyrol. Police Regts. 'Bozen', 'Alpenvorland', 'Schlander' and 'Brixen' were recruited between October 1943 and October 1944, and served all over occupied Italy.

In November 1944 new South Tyrolean forces were created as part of the Volkssturm—the 'home guard' organisation created throughout Reich territory from September 1944. The new units differed in some respects from the rest of the Volkssturm: they adopted a title—Standschutzen—in accordance with Tyrolean tradition; they wore their own armshield insignia; and they were organised by the Police, not by the Nazi Party. The three Standschutzen-Bataillone were named 'Meran', 'Gossensass' and 'Mals'. A separate force entitled Sudtiroler Ordnungsdienst (later retitled Stadt-und-Landwacht) was also recruited among *Volksdeutsche*; its total strength of some 18,000 men was made up of small local units.

In Italy the German Police recruited volunteer units, something not seen in other Western countries. The Corpo di Sicurezza Trentino, with a strength of about 1,000 Italians, served on attachment to the German Police in the South Tyrol. Another Italian unit was the so-called Miliz-Regiment 'De Maria' (Polizei), which would provide the main element for the Italian SS Brigade. In the Udine region the Sturmlegion M 'Tagliamento' (Polizei)—in Italian form, Legione d'Assalto M 'Tagliamento' (Polizia)—was employed against guerrillas. In January 1945 this unit was retitled Polizei-Freiwillige Gebirgsjäger Btl. 'Tagliamento' (Volunteer Police Alpine Bn. 'Tagliamento').

The German Police tried to attract to their ranks the efficient Carabinieri, Italy's traditional national gendarmerie force. They were not particularly successful in this, as the force had a strong Monarchist tradition; nevertheless, several Volunteer Police Battalions were created to incorporate them. The order of battle of the HSSPF 'Oberitalien' of February 1944 includes 11 Volun-

teer Police Bns. and two Volunteer Police Depot Bns. recruited among Italians. In April 1944 there were only four battalions and the two depot units. Finally, in December 1944, there were two Polizei-Freiwillige Btl. Italien, and one Polizei-Ersatz Btl. Italien.

The HSSPF 'Adriatisches Kustenland' was more successful in recruiting Italians: here the volunteers would not have to fight their compatriots in the resistance movements, but the Yugoslavian partisans who were seeking to annexe that border region of Italy. The June 1944 order of battle includes Police Bns. entitled 'Gorz', 'Udine', 'Fiume' and 'Pola'.

The **SD**—the SS Security Service—did not employ its Einsatzgruppen ('Action Groups') in Western Europe as it did in the East. Only small supervisory staffs were set up. In some individual cases Flemish, French, and other foreigners are believed to have volunteered for service with these groups.

The **Allgemeine-SS**, the black-clad 'general service' militia of the Nazi Party (not to be confused with the grey-uniformed Waffen-SS combat units) established national branches in the 'Germanic' occupied countries. They recruited the most active

Jonas Lie, here wearing Waffen-SS uniform, was Quisling's Minister of Justice and Police, and leader of the Norwegian Germanic SS. At right are two officers of this *Germanske-SS Norge* (note cuff title); the NS badge of an eagle clutching a 'St Olaf's Cross' can be seen on their left sleeves—and also as the cap badge of the Norwegian police officer behind Lie. (Neulen)

and committed collaborationists in Norway, Denmark, Flanders and Holland for this 'Germanic SS', which acted as a provider of volunteers for foreign Waffen-SS units and other pro-German security forces. The **Waffen-SS** itself set up some volunteer units with specifically security duties: SS Guard Bn. 3 'Nordwest' from Dutch volunteers, SS Guard Bn. 6 'Nord' from Norwegians, and SS Guard Bn. 'Sjaelland' from Danes.

Resistance in Western Europe centred on espionage and intelligence-gathering; and the Germans took active measures to counter these efforts. The responsible services were the **Abwehr**, or Wehrmacht Counter-Intelligence Service; and the **Geheime Feldpolizei**, GFP—the Secret Military Police. The Abwehr recorded important successes, particularly in Holland, where their efforts were aided by some appalling lapses of judgement on the part of the responsible British SOE department in London. In January 1944 all Abwehr personnel in Western Europe were reorganised into five units called Frontaufklärungskommando (Front Intelligence Commands): FAK 306, 307, 313, 314 and 350. The GFP, manned by former members of the German Criminal Police, operated under the orders of Army Groups or Military Commanders in the occupied countries. Members of this organisation served either in Army uniform or in civilian clothes; their mission was to combat espionage and sabotage against military targets.

The SOE

The history of Western European Resistance is unthinkable without a mention, however brief, of the British Special Operations Executive. Created in July 1940 by Winston Churchill, with the task of 'setting Europe ablaze', the SOE was led at first by Hugh Dalton, and later by Lord Wolmer. In practice, the organisation's mission was two-fold: to oblige the Wehrmacht to maintain large occupation forces in Western Europe, and to hamper the harnessing of European industry and economy to the German cause.

The history of each department of SOE is so complex that not even a brief summary may be

Norwegian *Milorg* members train somewhere in central Norway. Led by ex-Army officers, this organisation nevertheless carried out few attacks before 1945.

attempted here. Inevitably, there was some duplication of effort between various different British and Allied agencies concerned with the occupied countries; and inevitably, these agencies did not always see their best interests as entirely coincidental with those of others. In an underground war this kind of friction and internal rivalry can all too often lead to tragic and unnecessary deaths. SOE included both British and foreign personnel, in England and inserted behind enemy lines. Contacts with some of the 'governments-in-exile' and with resistance movements in occupied Europe were sometimes uneasy. The SOE was sometimes accused of acting mainly in the British interest, without taking account of the harm done locally; and of damaging the authority of the governments-in-exile.

In defence of SOE it can be stated with confidence that under the circumstances in which they had to operate no agency could have achieved much more. Their efforts were often hampered by deviousness on the part of other agencies and groups; in truth, many of the 'governments-in-exile' had little authority to *be* compromised; and resistance groups were quite ruthless in their attempts to enlist or manipulate SOE support to strengthen their local position against rival resistance groups.

What is certain is that SOE grew enormously. Excluding Italy, they sent into occupied Western Europe some 7,500 agents. Many of these brave men and women were captured, hideously tortured, and finally executed, or sent to concentration camps. Others, luckier in their assignments or contacts, found themselves responsible for the

Sentries at the doors of the headquarters of the Danish *Schalburg Korpset* wear Danish uniforms apart from the 'mobile swastika' collar patch and the steel helmet; cf. Plate C2. (Neulen)

logistic support of large resistance networks. They were the conduit through which clandestine RAF missions dropped money, arms, explosives, and signals equipment. In 1944 SOE had some 60 special schools where saboteurs, spies, radio operators, document forgers and other specialists were trained. From that year the SOE's leading rôle in this work declined relative to that of the American OSS (Office of Strategic Services). Commanding much greater resources, the OSS was able, for instance, to drop 1,200 tons of arms and equipment into occupied Italy between January and April 1945 alone.

Norway

Collaboration

For a long time it was believed that collaboration had already begun in Norway before the German occupation, and that Maj. Quisling's Fascist party—the **Nasjonal Samlig**—acted as a 'fifth column' during the invasion. In fact, it now appears that the NS did not so act: though Quisling—whose name has become synonymous with the idea of a paid traitor—did proclaim himself 'head of government', and order the Norwegian armed

forces to cease fire, to the surprise of the Germans and of his own followers.

Germany had planned that—following the Danish pattern—Norway's independent political system should remain in being, and the king remain in the country, to lend an air of legitimacy to an occupation concerned solely with preventing Allied landings. This scenario dissolved with Quisling's unexpected bid for power, and the consequent escape of King Haakon VII to England. It soon became clear that the only faction upon which the Germans could rely was Quisling's NS—a party which before the war had never attracted more than two per cent of the vote, nor ever elected a member to parliament. Nevertheless, during the first two years of occupation the membership of the NS grew to some 45,000. In February 1942 Germany made Quisling 'Minister-President' of Norway—exceptional treatment, among European collaborationist leaders. Quisling saw himself as leader of a country allied to Germany; but in reality, power was wielded by Reichskommissar Terboven. A gifted theorist, Vidkun Quisling was a complete failure as a practical politician, and never attracted the support of a significant number of Norwegians.

The NS had a series of political organisations, some uniformed—the political leaders' corps, women's and youth organisations, etc; and under the Quisling government several state organisations were brought into a close relationship with the NS—the para-military Labour Service and the re-organised police forces among them.

A further body, the NS militia, was titled the **Hird**—a term from Viking history. First raised in 1933, it was re-organised and re-uniformed after the occupation; and in March 1941 received police powers. The Hird was divided into seven regiments, plus naval and air sections (**Hirdmarinen** and **Hirden Flykorpset**—both organised during the war, and sources of volunteers for the Kriegsmarine and Luftwaffe). There was also the élite **Forergarden**, Quisling's bodyguard section. In March 1942 a single armed and barracked battalion was created, later named **Hirdens Bedriftsvern** ('Hird Factory Guard'); this unit adopted field grey uniform and other German items. As the Norwegian Resistance was never very active, the Hird did not need larger armed forces.

A Norwegian section of the German Allgemeine-SS was also created, known initially as the **Norges-SS** and later as the **Germanske-SS Norge**. Theoretically it was a branch of the Hird, but in fact the Norwegian SS was virtually autonomous and had direct links with the Germans. Never more than about 1,300 strong, in one battalion and several companies, they wore, after a transitional period, uniforms almost identical to those of the German Allgemeine-SS. The NS emblem, an eagle with the Cross of St Olaf, was used instead of German insignia; and the mountain cap was always worn, in place of the German *Schirmmütze*. In practice the Norwegian SS had little importance, as most members served either in the Waffen-SS unit or in the Norwegian Police.

Quisling re-organised and re-uniformed the Police. The **Ordenspoliti** and **Sikkerhetspoliti** were created, on the German model, with field grey uniforms bearing collar patches in green or black respectively; shoulder strap ranking was also of German inspiration. The cap badge resembled that of the NS and Hird, but with added oakleaves.

On 14 August 1943 the Hird, the Norwegian SS and the Police created by Quisling were integrated into the Norwegian armed forces.

Resistance

As time passed, resistance against the German occupiers became progressively stronger, due to several factors. From what started as a simple policy of preventive military occupation, the Germans moved towards a programme of imposition of the Nazi ideology. A series of initiatives launched by Quisling antagonised important sections of the population. The king's clear support for the Resistance was influential. In practical terms, the Resistance benefited from the relatively easy communications with England, which could be

An extraordinary sight in a country occupied by Nazi Germany: the Copenhagen general strike of June 1944. In one form or another the barricade displays most of the symbols employed by the Danish Resistance: the national flag, the Communist flag, the RAF's aircraft roundel marking, and a chalked 'C' enclosing an 'X'—for King Christian X.

reached by intrepid seamen taking small boats out of the unguardable thousands of inlets along the coast under cover of night and bad weather. The very long border with neutral Sweden was also useful, since the Swedes welcomed and protected resisters.

A regular fishing boat run from Britain, the so-called 'Shetland bus', helped bring weapons into Norway sufficient to equip 35,000 men. The Norwegian government-in-exile was also able to arrange for the military training in Sweden of a 'police force' of some 15,000. Despite this, the Norwegian Resistance was not particularly active.

The first resisters organised themselves in 1941 into the Military Organisation—**Milorg**—led mostly by ex-Army officers; sponsored from an early stage by SOE, it was at first not recognised by the government-in-exile. Nevertheless, early disagreement over methods led to a rupture with SOE. Milorg was determined to create a 'secret army' ready to act 'at the right moment'—i.e., when Allied forces landed to liberate Norway. The government-in-exile, socialist in complexion, was distrustful of the Milorg leadership; and the SOE was only interested in constant sabotage attempts. For these reasons the Norwegian Resistance was caught in something of an impasse. Until almost the end of the war most violent action against the Germans was the work of SOE and the Communist group **Norge Fritt**. Milorg's main contribution to the war was to tie down large German forces in Norway. The more active SOE saboteurs achieved important successes, of which the most important was undoubtedly the destruction of the Norsk Hydro 'heavy water' plant, necessary to Germany's atomic bomb research.

Milorg was eventually recognised by the government-in-exile, and the dispute with the SOE was patched up. By the end of the war they had some 40,000 men. The separate civil resistance organisation, **Sivorg**, was extremely successful in resisting Quisling's and Terboven's policy of imposing Nazi ideology. Unlike movements in other countries, the Norwegian Resistance did not have a policy of assassinating leaders of collaborationist groups—with very few exceptions, such as Karl Marthinsen, chief of police and supreme commander of the Hird, who was killed in February 1945.

When the German forces capitulated the Milorg rose up in arms all over the country, before the arrival of the British liberation forces. The Wehrmacht did not put up any resistance. Later came the 'purification' phase; and as one might expect of Norway, the combing out of collaborators was firm, but not cruel. Police files were opened on some 90,000 Norwegians deemed to have collaborated—a figure which should be seen against a total population of 3,000,000.

Denmark

The German occupation of Denmark took place smoothly, in accordance with plans long established, without either surprises (such as Quisling's intervention) or problems (such as King Haakon's escape). Occupied to serve as a base for military operations, Denmark was at first treated with extraordinary leniency. National sovereignty was respected in many of its aspects: neither the Danish armed forces, nor the police, nor the parliament, nor the courts of justice were disbanded, and Fascist political elements were not imposed on the government.

Before the war Denmark had several such parties, the most important being the DNSAP, the **Danmarks National-Socialistiske Arbajder Parti**, directed by Frits Clausen. Although reaping some small benefits from the occupation, the DNSAP remained unimportant; and the several

After the German surrender the *Danske Brigade*—**trained and equipped by the Swedes, but destined never to fight—returned to Denmark.**

other, competitive Fascist-leaning parties were quite insignificant. Germany did not place any weight on them, preferring the enthusiastic support of some members of the Danish government, notably Erik Scavenius, the Foreign Minister. He was responsible for Denmark joining the Anti-Komintern Treaty, and supported Danish volunteer recruitment for the Waffen-SS. Under these circumstances Germany did not appoint either a Reichskommissar or a Military Governor, but only a Reichsbevollmachtiger or 'plenipotentiary'.

Lacking either a government-in-exile, easy communications with England, or any suitable terrain for guerrilla operations, Denmark was inevitably slow to get effective resistance under way. Unsurprisingly, the first steps were taken by the Communists and by SOE men. The Danish Communist Party was outlawed by the government shortly after the invasion of Russia; the Communists responded vigorously, forming the first armed group, the **Borgerlige Partisaner** or BOPA. They probably did more damage to the Danish economy than to Germany's war effort; but it must be admitted that the riskiest operations were carried out by BOPA men—e.g. the attacks on military and police barracks to get arms, since they were not supplied by SOE. Non-Communist resistance got under way only from mid-1942, with the appearance of the Social Democrat **Ringen**, Christian **Dansk Samlig** and, in autumn 1943, **Holger Danske** groups.

This increasing resistance, and their generally declining fortunes, led the Germans to stiffen their occupation policy. In March 1943, after victory for the Democratic parties in the Danish elections, there were strikes and demonstrations. The Germans responded by disbanding the Danish Armed forces. In September the various resistance movements formed the Denmark Liberation Committee, which included a member of the SOE's Danish section: the committee's main task was to form a 'secret army' for 'the right moment'. With the same goal, a military unit termed the Danske Brigade, nearly 5,000 strong, was recruited and organised on Swedish territory.

The collaborationists did not remain passive. Since the DNSAP had proved ineffective, the initiative was passed to the Danish veterans of the Waffen-SS. The last commander of the Waffen-SS

The German *Reichskommissar* in Holland, Dr Artur Seyss-Inquart, meets German and Dutch Police officers. The latter still wear the old uniform, later changed for a more Germanic look with the creation of the new 'Communal Police'.

Frikorps Danmark created in April 1943 the **Schalburg Korpset**, named after a previous commander killed fighting in Russia. It was organised as a Danish branch of the Germanic SS, but, alone among the national organisations, it never adopted the 'SS' designation. The Schalburg Korpset recruited Eastern Front veterans and the most active collaborators; its 700 men were divided into five companies, and an intelligence section known by the initials 'ET'. They wore either khaki Danish Army uniform, or black uniform directly inspired by the Allgemeine-SS. They adopted the same techniques as the resistance groups, and responded to each resistance assassination with one of their own. It was said at the time that every act of sabotage provoked a 'schalburgtage'.

The Wehrmacht also raised auxiliary security units in Denmark. From February 1943 a unit entitled the **Marinevaegtere** was recruited by the Kriegsmarine. This 1,500-man corps was armed, and wore dark blue uniforms and German helmets, and the German eagle and swastika insignia. From that April the Luftwaffe raised Danish and Schleswig *Volksdeutsche* airfield security units designated **Flugplatzkommandos**, who wore Luftwaffe uniform with a yellow brassard reading '*Den Tyske Vaernemagt Kombatenterne*' ('Combatant of the German Armed Forces'). A very active collaborator, Capt. Paul Sommer, who had flown with the Luftwaffe, raised a separate 'Guard Corps of the German Air Force in Denmark'—**Vagtkorpset det Tyske Luftvaaben in Danmark**, usually called simply the Sommers Vagtkorps; with about 1,200 men, this unit wore Luftwaffe uniform. The total strength of these four organisations was about 4,000—quite an impressive figure, given that the Danish forces numbered only 6,600 effectives in 1939.

Spontaneous demonstrations and strikes took place in June 1944 in protest against the imposition of a curfew by the Germans. These were immediately supported by the Liberation Committee, who announced a general strike. The Germans, aided by the Schalburg Corps, encircled Copenhagen; but in the end a negotiated settlement was reached, one of its terms being the withdrawal of the Schalburg Corps. In September the Germans disbanded the Danish police. In their place they created the **Hipo Korpset** or Auxiliary Police Corps, using the Schalburg Corps 'ET' section as the basis. Their black uniform, similar to that of the Schalburg Corps, bore the Danish police insignia. This organisation was heavily committed against the Danish Resistance; and their commander, Eriksen, was assassinated in February 1945. The Schalburg Corps itself was completely transformed, becoming first SS Training Bn. 'Schalburg', and finally SS Guard Bn. 'Sjaelland'.

The secret army organised by the Liberation Committee grew steadily, and by the end of 1944 had 25,000 men; this figure had risen to 45,000 by the time of the German surrender. The SOE, which enjoyed good relations with the Danish Resistance, helped to equip them. After the Allied victory the Liberation Committee was recognised as the *de facto* government. In the 'purification' phase, some 16,000 Danes were arrested for collaboration.

Holland

Collaboration

As in the case of Norway, the royal family and the government escaped and took refuge in Britain. The Germans appointed a Reichskommissar, Seyss-Inquart, to rule the country. Initially it even seemed that they could rely upon the co-operation

February 1943, The Hague: Mussert's bodyguard, the *Lijfwacht v.d.Leider*, at Gen. Seyffardt's funeral. Note all-black uniform, including shirt; German-style belt (with 'wolf hook' buckle device) and pistol holster; NSB arm badge; and cuff title bearing the name of this militia in script. (Neulen)

of the Democratic politicians. The prime minister of the government-in-exile, D. J. Geer, left London and returned to Holland via Lisbon to argue for co-operation with the occupiers. A non-Fascist party with the same programme, the Nederlandse Unie, was created after the occupation, and attracted 800,000 members.

Eventually the Germans decided to rely upon the local Fascists, of which there had been several parties before the war. The most important was the **Nationaal-Socialistische Beweging**, NSB, led by Anton Mussert. Unlike its Norwegian and Danish counterparts the NSB enjoyed genuine popular support—300,000 votes in the 1935 municipal elections. After the occupation the Democratic parties were disbanded, and other Fascist parties were obliged to join the NSB.

Mussert's party was completely uniformed. It included a Political Leadership Corps, a Speakers' Corps, and many trade, youth, and women's sections. The NSB also had militia organisations:

the **Weer Afdeelingen** ('Defence Sections') and **Lijfwacht** (Mussert's bodyguard). A Dutch branch of the Germanic SS, called at first the **Nederlandsche-SS** and subsequently the **Germansche-SS en Nederland**, joined them. The militias, like the whole NSB, wore black uniforms.

The WA was organised in nine units called Heerban (one of them actually based in Germany). It also had motorised, naval, cavalry, flying, and signal branches; officers' and NCOs' schools; and a reserve organisation. In 1942 the WA received 'police powers in emergency situations'. The Lijfwacht van der Leider, differentiated by colour patch colour, was much smaller. The Dutch Germanic SS had five regiments and a police regiment; in theory it answered to the NSB, but in practice to the Germans.

The Germans re-organised the Dutch police, creating the 'Communal Police' to replace the municipal forces of the major cities. Organised along military lines, this service wore black uniforms with closed collars bearing blue patches with silver star and bar rank insignia. The peaked cap bore an oval cockade in national colours with a flaming grenade at the top and an oakleaf spray at the bottom. Trained by the German SS, this force initially had a strength of some 3,000 men.

Other collaborationist security forces included: the **Vrijvillige Hulp Politie**, with similar tasks to the British special constabulary, and a strength of several thousand; the **Kontroll Kommando**, responsible for controlling forced labour workers, who wore field grey with black collar patches bearing the letters 'KK'; and, from 1943, the **Wachtabteilung**, consisting of older men acting as factory and military installation watchmen, wearing a uniform similar to the German Police but with a German Army eagle-and-swastika badge and a Dutch armshield.

The most important collaborationist security force was the Landwacht, later Landstorm. Created in 1943 as the **Landwacht Nederland**, it recruited the fittest men from the NSB, the WA and the Dutch Germanic SS. In October 1943, retitled **Landstorm Nederland**, it came under the control of the SS. The following month a second Landwacht was created under NSB control, incorporating all remaining NSB and WA men of

Initially the Dutch *Landstorm* retained the uniforms of the organisations from which recruits came; here, we see a Dutch Germanic SS-man (left) and two WA men, all in black. The SS-man has black-and-silver piped collar patches, an SS belt buckle and a plain cuff band. The WA man at right is a *Wachtmeester*, with two bronze bars of rank on his scarlet collar patches. Note the Dutch lion decal on the German helmets. (Neulen)

military age. There was a permanent element of some 3,000 men, and a part-time element of about 8,000. Initially both Landstorm and Landwacht wore the black uniforms of their parent organisations—the WA, SS, and Communal Police; or arm brassards on civilian clothes.

Field grey uniforms were progressively introduced, particularly in the Landstorm. Both forces adopted the NSB's traditional 'wolf hook' insignia; and also the flaming grenade badge of the Communal Police, which was worn as a collar patch device and replaced the SS death's-head on the cap. The Landstorm fought against the Dutch Resistance, and to some extent against British airborne troops around Arnhem in October 1944. It was eventually amalgamated with other Dutch personnel, e.g. the SS Guard Bn. 'Nordwest', in the so-called 34th SS-Freiwilligen Grenadier-Division 'Landstorm Nederland'.

Resistance
The Dutch Resistance encountered serious problems. The German security forces accomplished some very successful coups against them; their leaders had difficulty co-ordinating their efforts; and, from the start, there were disagreements between the Dutch section of SOE and the secret service created by the Dutch government-in-exile.

The first group, founded in 1940, was the **Orde**

Dienst, largely directed by ex-Army officers, and with the limited objective of preparing themselves to keep order when the Germans were eventually forced to evacuate Holland. The Communists were, as always, more radical, and mounted direct attacks on Germans and collaborators; but their numerical weakness prevented their causing the occupiers any very serious problems.

That the Orde Dienst had contact with SOE proved to be a disastrous disadvantage. In November 1941 the Abwehr detained a number of Dutch SOE agents, and in the course of their interrogation gained access to their radio links with SOE in London. There were extraordinary lapses of security and of judgement both in Holland and in London; and as a result, communications between London, the Orde Dienst and other resistance groups were disastrously compromised and manipulated by the Germans for a long period. This Operation 'Nordpol'—also called the 'Englandspiel', or 'England Game'—brought the Germans enough equipment, weapons and money to equip about 10,000 resisters, dropped innocently into their waiting hands by the RAF. It cost the lives of many RAF aircrew; and the capture, interrogation, and in many cases the wretched death of no less than 450 SOE agents and local activists. The 'England Game' only came to an end late in 1943, as a result of the incredibly courageous escape of an SOE man from detention and all the way back to England. By that time the Dutch Resistance had suffered damage from which it never really recovered.

There were several attempts to frustrate the occupiers, even so. There was a general strike in February 1941—the first time this had happened in a German-occupied country. The Communists carried out important missions, such as the assassination of Gen. Seyffardt, the former Dutch Army chief of staff and sponsor of the Dutch Waffen-SS Legion. The chief of the German security forces, SS-Gen. Reuter, escaped an attempt on his life; but many lesser NSB and WA men were killed. The main effort of the Resistance went into helping the so-called 'onderduikers' or 'submerged people'—men and women hiding out from the Germans. Several organisations were involved, notably the **Landelijke Knokploegen**, LK.

An attempt was made to rebuild the Resistance

after the 'England Game' finished. The SOE and the government-in-exile's **Bureau Bijzondere Opdrachten**, BBO, overcame the difficulties between them. The OD, LK, and Raad van Verzet ('Resistance Council') were brought together as the **Nederlandse Binnelandse Strijdkrachten** ('Dutch Home Forces') under the authority of Prince Bernhardt. In truth, however, an effective unity was not achieved; the Resistance did not have the men or the weapons to help the Allied armies on the battlefield in the late phase of the war. The civil organisation was relatively efficient, as has been mentioned; they fermented another general strike in 1943 to protest against the internment of Dutch Army personnel who had been freed in 1940, and in September 1944 railwaymen brought traffic to a halt in support of Operation 'Market Garden'.

Wachtmeester **of the** *Fabriekswacht* **(the future** *Wachtbrigade***) in the first model uniform, worn after its integration in the** *Dietsche Militie*. **Shoulder straps and two-point collar patches are green. The main difference between this and the DM/ZW uniform was the cap. The** *Fabriekswacht* **wore a wreathed 'wolf hook' rune below a seamew clutching the VNV triangle-in-a-circle badge, shaped to resemble the eagle of the Luftwaffe, the sponsoring service of the** *Fabriekswacht*. **(Vincx)**

At the end of the war some 50,000 Dutch were prosecuted for their service in German or pro-German armed organisations; some 15,000 of these men had served in those forces formed for anti-resistance operations.

Belgium

Belgium had suffered German occupation in the First World War, and in some ways the experience of 1940–44 provided parallels. The Military Governor of Belgium and Northern France, Gen. Alexander von Falkenhausen, was the nephew of Gen. Ludwig von Falkenhausen, Belgium's Military Governor in 1914–18. Many of those who worked against the occupiers in 1940–44 were risking their lives in the same cause for the second time; and the main collaborationist tendency was—as in 1914–18—to be found among the Flemish nationalists. The situation in Belgium was complicated not only by the existence of two distinct national communities—the Flemish and the French-speaking Walloons, who generally held very different views on most subjects; but by the fact that although the government had taken ship for England, the king chose to stay in Belgium.

Resistance

In strictly military terms the Belgian Resistance was never very strong, and always divided. In 1940–41 a number of movements were created, dedicated to armed action 'when the right moment came'. Some were regional: the **Armée de la Libération** in Liège, the **Witte Brigade** in Antwerp, **Les Insoumis** in Hainault, **Groupe C** in Brussels, etc. (The last-named, mainly consisting of engineering school students, was to be very effective in industrial sabotage.)

Other movements had a national basis. The **Mouvement National Belge** was led by Camille Joset, a First World War resistance veteran; it engaged in intelligence-gathering and propaganda work as well as sabotage. Joset and his main lieutenants were arrested in 1942. The **Légion Belge** was made up of Army reserve officers and was led by Col. Bastin, a minister of the government-in-exile. He managed to link the

Légion Belge with the **Mouvement National Royaliste**, and was negotiating with the Witte Brigade and the Armée de la Libération when his arrest by the Germans defeated this attempt to unify the resistance groups.

The Communists were very effective. Their **Armée Belge des Partisans du Front de l'Indépendance et de la Libération** was credited with killing some 500 German personnel in the Brussels region in 1941–44; and from 1942 to 1944 they killed about 1,000 Belgian collaborators.

The government-in-exile called all these groups collectively the '**Armée Secrète**', but after Bastin's arrest no such unified organisation actually existed. The defence ministry of the London government had separate links with each group. They tried to limit the Communist FIL to civil resistance, but this movement had, as mentioned, its own armed action groups; they were in fact the only partisans to attack

An NCO of the 1st Bn., *Vlaamse Wacht*—cf. Plate E2. He displays his battalion number on cap and right breast; collar patches were plain for all ranks, but note *Tresse*; exact ranking was worn on the shoulder straps. (Vincx)

the withdrawing German troops in the Ardennes late in 1944.

Allied planners expected the Belgian Resistance to rise in support of the Allied advance, but this insurrection never took place. Although the Secret Army had some 45,000 members by 1944, only about 7,000 were armed. The German retreat was carried out very quickly; on 2 September 1944 all resistance forces were placed under Gen. Gérard's authority, but this had few practical consequences, as Allied troops occupied the whole country within a few days. One of the most strategically valuable resistance operations was to prevent the Germans from demolishing the vital port of Antwerp. The Belgian Resistance forces were not transformed—as was the case in France and Italy—into regular Army units after the German evacuation.

The civil side of the Resistance was much more effective. It was co-ordinated by the Ministry of Justice, Information and Propaganda, and achieved brilliant results in information-gathering and espionage. Groups such as the **Union des Patriotes Belges** and the **Comité d'Entraide** specialised in organising escape and evasion routes to Spain, which carried many Allied airmen to safety. The 'Clarence-Cleveland' network was established by W. Dewe, First World War director of the Dame Blanche group; Dewe was killed by the

July 1944, Brussels: men of the *Wachtbrigade* swear allegiance to Hitler. They wear a mixture of items: DM tunic, trousers and shirt, Luftwaffe belt and helmet, and SS-style collar patches. Again, note Flemish arm shield—a black lion on a yellow shield. (Vincx)

Germans while trying to escape arrest, but many other networks—some 35 in all—remained in being. More than 10,000 men and women were involved in this work, and the SOE and the Belgian government-in-exile sent some 300 agents into the country.

Collaboration

It is important to distinguish between the regions of Flanders and Wallonia. Flanders had the highest proportion of collaborators in the whole of Western Europe. A powerful separatist party, the **Vlaamsch Nationaal Verbond**, VNV, practised an active pro-German policy and followed Fascist ideology. With 100,000 members, led at first by De Clerq and later by Dr Elias, the VNV was recognised by the Germans as the only party in Flanders. It had several uniformed branches, including a militia, the **Dietsche Militie**, DM.

The militia was divided into four branches. The main one was the **DM/Zwarte Brigade**, 12,000 strong, and organised in five Heerban. Their leader, R. Tollenaere, died fighting with the SS in Russia. Black Brigade members often acted as Hilfsfeldgendarmerie ('Auxiliary Military Police') wearing German brassards. The **DM/Motor Brigade**, who wore the same uniform as the DM/ZB, disappeared in 1943 when the majority of members joined Transport Regts. of the German NSKK. The **DM/Hulp Brigade** was an auxiliary organisation of elderly men, and wore a simpler uniform. The fourth main branch was the **Wachtbrigade**, which had a more complex history.

Raised in May 1941 as the **Fabriekwacht** or 'Factory Guard', sponsored by the Luftwaffe and collaborationist elements, it was retitled in early 1942 **Vlaamse Fabriekwacht**, and linked to the VNV; now part of the DM, it wore DM/ZB uniform with minor differences. In June 1943 it received its definitive title, **Vlaamse Wachtbrigade**. The uniform included Luftwaffe, SS and DM items. Its total strength of some 4,000 men was organised in 14 companies and thence into four battalions. In July 1944 it was transformed into a Luftwaffe Flak Brigade[1].

The small Flemish branch of the Germanic SS, created in 1940, had no links with the VNV and

[1]See MAA 147, *Foreign Volunteers of the Wehrmacht 1941–45.*

depended entirely on the radical Devlag group, a collaborationist movement which called for the incorporation of Flanders into the Reich. The **Germaansche-SS in Vlaanderen** raised only a single regiment, most of whose members ended up fighting in Russia after joining the Waffen-SS. The Germanic SS uniform was virtually identical to that of the German Allgemeine-SS.

In Wallonia the Fascist political party led by Léon Degrelle, the **Rex**, had been falling into decline; the occupation revived it somewhat, although it was never as strong as the VNV in Flanders. August 1940 saw the Rex form uniformed militia sections for the first time—the **Formations de Combat**, dressed in dark blue shirt, tunic and trousers, and later in a sort of dark blue overall. The Formations de Combat included a motorised branch, the Brigade Volante Rex; most of its members subsequently enlisted in the NSKK. The Formations de Combat were also phased out in 1943, as most members were fighting in Russia with the Légion Wallonie[1] or in other units.

[1]See MAA 147; also MAA 34, *The Waffen-SS* (Revised Edition)

A *Garde Wallone* **second lieutenant and his men of the 1st Bn.; only the officer wears an open collar and tie. Note the NCO at right, with a German belt, and white rank stripes round his cuffs;** *Tresse* **was worn on the collar only after the end of 1943, when rank insignia moved to the shoulder straps. The uniform piping is red; and the helmets are the Belgian Army model. (Centre de Recherches et d'Etudes de la SGM)**

Under the control of the German military authorities two armed auxiliary security forces were created. In Flanders the **Vlaamse Wacht** (*n.b.*, not to be confused with the DM's Vlaamse Wacht-brigade, above) recruited from June 1941 among Flemish ex-soldiers, with the support of the VOS veterans' association, and later of the VNV. After a period in Belgian Army khaki the Vlaamse Wacht changed to dark blue uniforms, exchanged for German field grey in June 1944. The four battalions, comprising 13 Rifle Companies, two Railway Guard Companies, one Channel Guard Company and two Depot Companies, totalled about 4,000 men.

In July 1941 the equivalent **Garde Wallone** was raised, from Rex members and Walloon veterans. There were two battalions, one of them responsible for guarding the railway system. They wore the same uniform as the Vlaamse Wacht, except for different cockade colours; the use of red instead of yellow uniform piping; and the use of the Adrian, rather than the Dutch Army steel helmet used by the Flemings.

Other auxiliary forces were the Belgian **Gendarmerie** and the Rural Guard. Maintaining its traditional uniform, the Gendarmerie—divided by the Germans into Flemish and Walloon sections—created special mobile units to fight the Resistance; VNV and Rex members were recruited into the service, or attached as auxiliaries. The Rural Guard (**Boerenwacht** or **Garde Rurale**, respectively, in Flanders and Wallonia) was created in June 1941 by the collaborationist-controlled farmers' and food distributors' corporation, to protect crops and barns against sabotage. After some members were killed the Guard received uniforms and weapons. By May 1942 it had 28,000 men in Flanders and 38,000 in Wallonia; many were conscripts, who wore only arm brassards in place of the Guard's dark green uniform. Despite its important size this was not a significant branch of the collaborationist forces; for many of its members it was a straightforward means

The *Garde Rurale/Boerenwacht*; the insignia—see collar— was a sword between two ears of corn, and the first lieutenant displays his rank insignia of two 'pips' below this. The sergeant-major's rank is indicated by cuff bars. (Centre de Recherches et d'Etudes de la SGM)

of protecting their livelihood, innocent of ideological meaning.

At the end of the war some 87,000 Belgians were accused of collaboration. No less than 4,000 were condemned to death, though relatively few sentences were actually carried out. In Belgium, unlike the countries described in earlier chapters, the official 'purification' process was accompanied by an unofficial campaign of vengeance by the Resistance, in which many people were summarily killed.

France

France presents a more complex picture, both of Resistance and of Collaboration, than any other European country.

After the short campaign of May/June 1940 the French Army considered itself defeated; and the legally appointed head of government, Marshal Pétain, signed an armistice with Germany. The Germans would occupy the northern and Atlantic coastal regions, under the supreme authority of a Militär Befehlshaber in Frankreich. The rest of France, the so-called Free Zone, together with the French overseas empire, remained under the control of Pétain's government, whose seat was at Vichy.

Officially, the Vichy government collaborated with the Germans; but in fact they never declared war on Britain, despite the fact that British ships had attacked the French fleet at anchor, and that British troops had occupied some parts of the French empire in hard fighting. The Vichy regime was not Fascist; the majority of its members practised towards Germany an ambiguous policy of '*attentisme*'—'wait and see'.

Vichy was assailed by more radical groups at both ends of the spectrum. Gen. de Gaulle took refuge in Britain, and—though his legitimacy rested on little more than a few weeks' tenure of a very junior ministerial post in a fallen government—he established himself by sheer force of character as the leader of the 'Free French' movement. (Although it was to be three years before his leadership of France was to be finally agreed by Britain and America; and for much of that time his actual resources were little greater than one brigade.)

Meanwhile, in occupied Paris, several Fascist groups carried out a very active programme of collaboration, and attacked Vichy's lukewarm *attentisme*. To confuse the picture even further, it must be pointed out that the different Fascist parties also fought among themselves—as, indeed, did the different resistance movements which gradually emerged. If the realities of life in an occupied country give the lie to the simplicities of Hollywood, how much more is that true of a half-occupied, half-sovereign country.

France was authorised to maintain an 'Armistice Army' of 100,000 men, and its Navy. Most officers, loyal to Vichy, were nevertheless hostile to Germany. When the Allies landed in French North Africa in November 1942, to a generally friendly reception from the French colonial forces, the Germans occupied the Free Zone; the Armistice Army was disbanded, and the Navy was scuttled.

A special case was the Légion Tricolore, formed in June 1942 and disbanded a few months later; it included the LVF[1], which thus far had not received any official support from Vichy. The Légion Tricolore was supported by the most radical ministers, who considered it the most col-

Vichy Premier Laval inspecting the *Légion Tricolore*, summer 1942. They wear French Army khaki uniforms with Fortress Troops berets; on the right breast is a khaki shield-shaped patch displaying a Napoleonic eagle with a shield in national colours on its chest. (Neulen)

laborationist of all Army units. A special breast badge was worn. In July 1943 there was formed, to take the place of the disbanded Armistice Army, a unit designated 1st Regiment 'Royal Auvergne'. There were also railway flak units, created in April 1943 from ex-Armistice Army members, to provide anti-aircraft defence for the railway system; about 10,000 strong, they wore French Air Force uniform.

It should be noted that no organised units of the French armed forces took part in operations against the French Resistance.

The same cannot be said of the French police forces. Vichy created new, specialised police branches with such meaningful titles as the Police for Jewish Affairs, and the Anti-Communist Police Service. Vichy's special police brigades were highly dedicated and efficient, and worked closely with the German SD. Within the retitled National Police, the Security Police branch (Police de Sûreté) were concerned with 'political crimes'. The 10,000 men of the **Groupes Mobiles de Reserve**, GMR, were directly concerned with anti-Resistance operations.

[1] See MAA 147, *Foreign Volunteers of the Wehrmacht 1941–45.*

There were also more static protection services such as the **Garde des Voies et des Communications** ('Roads and Communications'), and the **Gardes Méssiers** ('Harvest Guards'). All these police forces served in the Occupied and Free Zones alike.

Vichy had its own labour service, the Chantiers de la Jeunesse; and also supported a number of different youth organisations, e.g. the Compagnons de la France, the Jeunesses de France et d'Outre-Mer, etc. Pétain made use of these uniformed paramilitary groups, but many of their members detested the Germans. A more important source of assistance against internal opposition was the **Légion Française des Combatants** (later, '. . . et des Volontaires de la Révolution Nationale'). Made up of war veterans, and supporters of Vichy's so-called 'revolution', it totalled some million and a half members—though its active strength was much smaller. The élite among its several branches was the **Service d'Ordre Légionnaire**, SOL; they wore special brassards and badges on the Légion's uniform of khaki shirt and black or dark blue trousers, tie and beret. It was

the SOL which would later evolve into the much more efficient **Milice Française**.

Meanwhile, in London, Gen. de Gaulle created a 'French National Council' and the so-called 'Free French Forces', FFL; but his initial support inside France was insignificant. The real beginning of resistance activity came—as always—with Communist activism after the German invasion of Russia in June 1941. The very large and powerful French Communist Party had done all it could to damage the national war effort in 1940; now, it decided to attack the Wehrmacht—though rather to cause a spiral of terror and counter-terror than in expectation of doing the Germans any serious military harm.

The Communist Party created the Front National, an open organisation which was, however, firmly under Communist control; and an armed group, the **Franc-Tireurs et Partisans**, FTP. Many other organisations began to emerge. The most important in the Occupied Zone were **Libération Nord**, the **Organisation Civil et Militaire**, **Ceux de la Libération**, the **Armée des Volontaires**, the **Bataillons de la Mort** and the **Mouvement Nationale Révolutionnaire**. In the Free Zone the main groups were **Libération Sud**, **Franc-Tireur**, **Libérer et Fédérer**, **France d'Abord**, **Le Coq Enchainé**, **France au Combat**; and, within the Armistice Army, the **Organisation de Resistance de l'Armée**.

Several factors explain the relative importance of the French Resistance. Simplest and most important was the question of geography: France was bigger, emptier, and more suitable in all respects for clandestine activity on a large scale than her neighbours. Gen. de Gaulle was an inspirational and energetic leader. The French Communist Party was an important political force, with an existing infrastructure which took account of the need for security and conspiracy. The existence of the Free Zone was of inestimable advantage, providing an active sanctuary. Finally, the Germans made particularly serious errors in applying their occupation policies in France. The massive deportations from Alsace-Lorraine caused much bitterness; and the compulsory labour round-ups for German factories drove many young men into the mountains, and—in both senses—into the *maquis*.

The men mainly responsible for the fight against the French Resistance: the Higher SS and Police Leader for France, SS-Gruppenführer Oberg, and *Milice* leader Darnand. Around them are officers of the SD, German Police and *Milice*; between their heads can be seen an SS-Gruppenführer und Generalleutnant der Polizei wearing the new SS-style collar patches—see Plate A3.

From London the French section of SOE supervised its own information and sabotage networks, and collaborated with some resistance groups. SOE's relationship with Gen. de Gaulle's secret service, the Bureau Central de Renseignements et d'Action, BCRA, was particularly stormy.

Gradually, the different resistance groups began to acknowledge de Gaulle's leadership in the national struggle. In March 1943 his representative in France, Jean Moulin, managed to unify the major groups in the Free Zone under the title **Mouvements Unis de la Résistance**. Their armed groups, collectively termed l'Armée Secrète, were led by Gen. Delestraint. Shortly afterwards the Conseil National de la Résistance was created, initially under the chairmanship of Moulin and, after his arrest (he was to die under interrogation) under that of Georges Bidault. The Council included representatives of the armed groups, the political parties, the trade unions, etc; and had links with the Communists, who appeared to acknowledge, if grudgingly, that de Gaulle's supremacy

Three men of the *Franc Garde Permanente* in the *Milice Française* HQ in Paris. Rank bars are worn on the shoulder straps; and the *milicien* at left displays his unit number on collar patches. The *gamma*-and-sword badge on his left breast is that of the *École d'Uriage*, the *Milice* military academy. The *gamma* badge is worn on the beret—which was, correctly, pulled to the left—and the right breast. (Littlejohn)

was valid. (Though they continued to infiltrate, and manipulate, other groups.)

Apart from the armed resistance activities co-ordinated by the National Resistance Council's Committee for Military Action, many other clandestine activities were undertaken—propaganda, espionage networks, escape networks for refugees and Allied flyers, etc.

In opposing the Resistance the German security agencies were often successful at a local level. On several occasions they managed to replace captured French SOE agents with their own 'plants', with disastrous consequences for such networks as 'Interallié', 'Prosper', etc. At other times they took advantage of internal hostilities within the Resistance. They also made use of the various French

Miliciens of the *Franc Garde* training with small arms; note that some lack the breast badge and shoulder straps. The beret was widely used by Vichy collaborators, because the Germans had forbidden its use in Alsace-Lorraine.

Fascist parties. The main Fascist groups were:

The **Parti Populaire Français**, led by Doriot; his militia was at first termed the **Service d'Ordre**, later the **Gardes Françaises**.

The **Rassemblement National Populaire**, led by Deat; the RNP militia was the **Légion Nationale Populaire**.

The **Parti Franciste**, led by Bucard; his militia was first termed the **Corps Franc**, later the **Légion Franciste**.

There were also minor parties such as the Mouvement Social Révolutionnaire and the Ligue Française, and youth organisations like the Jeunes de l'Europe Nouvelle. All these movements, more or less, wore dark blue uniform shirts; and armed themselves on an individual basis as the Resistance became more active—sometimes from German sources. It was not unknown for the Fascist militias to fight among themselves; but they all belonged to the so-called 'National Anti-Terrorist Movement', and were at the disposal of the authorities.

The most active collaborationist organisation created by the Vichy government was the **Milice Française**, raised in 1943 and led by Darnand. There were youth and women's sections, but the main branch was the **Franc Garde**. This had two elements: a 5,000-strong permanent force, and a part-time force of about 8,000. The Milice had its own military academy, and 'Special Security Groups'. Dressed in dark blue tunics, trousers and berets, khaki shirts and black ties, and sometimes black-painted Adrian helmets, they used the white Greek letter *gamma* in a circle as a cap and breast insignia. They carried military small arms of French or captured Allied types.

The Franc Garde first saw action in Haut Savoie in spring 1943; and in December that year they began operations in the old Occupied Zone in the north. They took part in many fierce combats with the Resistance. Early in 1944, on the Glières plateau, a combined force of Wehrmacht, GMR police and Franc Garde personnel totally wiped out an important Resistance redoubt. January 1944 saw Darnand named 'General Secretary for Maintenance of Order' by the Vichy government.

Other minor collaborationist forces were:

The **Légion Nordafricaine**, made up of Muslims living in France; they wore uniforms similar to those of the Milice.

The **Milice Perrot** (in Breton, 'Bezenn Perrot'), made up of extremist Breton separatists; they wore field grey.

The **Kriegsmarine Wehrmanner** and **Kriegswerftpolizei La Pallice**, both raised by the German Navy and wearing Kriegsmarine blue with the yellow eagle and swastika. (The La Pallice U-boat base protection force wore it on the left upper arm, however, above the usual '*Im dienst der deutschen Wehrmacht*' brassard.)

Members of the German Navy security force, the *Kriegsmarine Wehrmanner*, attending a collaborationist congress. We know little about their uniform, and nothing about their rank insignia—from this group photo it seems clear that the silver(?) collar braid did not identify a particular rank. The gilt anchor on the shoulder strap may be a rank device. All wear the German Navy's yellow national eagle breast badge.

As the Allied invasion approached, the Resistance stepped up its activities. From spring 1944 onwards the Military Committee of the National Resistance Council directed all sabotage operations. The air-dropping of weapons and other equipment by SOE, OSS and BCRA increased; by D-Day enough had been received to arm 20,000 men fully, and 50,000 partially—and large caches of French weapons hidden in 1940 were also being issued. There was detailed planning of military operations on a wide scale to help the Allied landing forces: Operation 'Green', to sabotage communications; 'Blue', to sabotage electric power supplies; and Operation 'Turtle', to delay the movement of German reinforcements towards the beachheads. Many Allied 'Jedburgh' teams were parachuted into France before the invasion, to help co-ordinate resistance activity; and after the landings Allied special forces, such as the British SAS in their armed jeeps, penetrated enemy lines and co-operated with local resistance groups in quite large-scale fighting against German lines of communication and reinforcements. All these operations contributed significantly to the success of Operation 'Overlord'.

After the Normandy landings the Resistance, now grouped under the title **Forces Françaises de l'Interieur**, FFI, and under the command of Gen. Koenig, became directly involved in the battles of the Liberation. In some cases, as in Brittany, they were successful; in others, the results were tragic. The best-known defeat took place on the plateau of Vercors, where a brave but premature rising by one of the best prepared of all groups (they had received sponsorship from SOE at the rate of 2,300 francs per man per month, instead of the usual 600 francs) was finally crushed with

Spanish Republicans exiled after the Civil War played an active part in the Resistance in southern France. Here a group of them parade after the liberation of Toulouse, behind the red, yellow and purple Republican tricolour (repeated in miniature on the brassards—left). Uniforms and field equipment are of mixed origins, including some American webbing. Rifles and helmets are German, and one man carries a Sten. The captain and first lieutenant at far left wear French-style rank *galons* on chest patches.

The ugly side of the Liberation: women who were accused of consorting with their occupiers had their heads shaved. Other collaborators suffered a much more permanent fate during the wild days of the 'Purification'. The Resistance man on the right wears a tricolour brassard bearing a black Cross of Lorraine, and carries a Sten and a Mauser bayonet.

Photographed at the time of the German surrender in Paris, two Resistance fighters study a copy of the underground newspaper *L'Espoir*. The first lieutenant displays his two rank bars on his beret. The *resistante*, carrying both a rifle and a Thompson SMG, wears what appears to be a de-badged German summer combat tunic in reed-green denim.

military men and civil servants who had remained loyal to Vichy—France's legal government, let it be remembered; about 40,000 people were imprisoned, and many death sentences were passed by the new courts. There was also a great deal of killing without any form of legal process. Official figures suggest that there were about 10,000 summary executions of those accused of collaboration; other sources have suggested that the true figure may be nearer 100,000 deaths. Doubtless, many of these killings were justified; equally doubtless, many were squalid and opportunist murders.

great loss of life by SS and airborne troops. The FFI encircled and bottled up several German garrisons (e.g. Toulouse, Marseille, Toulon, Grenoble); and throughout France they disarmed and took prisoner thousands of German troops isolated and confused by the Allied advances from Normandy and Provence. The climax came with the rising in Paris itself, which might have ended tragically if Allied troops had not arrived on 24 August. Finally, the FFI units were transformed into regular units of the French Army; some were employed on garrison duties in France, while others got a chance to carry the fight into Germany.

The Liberation was immediately followed by a settling of scores. There was a widespread purge of

Italy

Resistance did not begin in Italy until the fall of Mussolini's Fascist regime, and the consequent occupation by Germany, in 1943. Yet it was in Italy that the fiercest guerrilla war was fought, by the most powerful forces.

The anti-Fascist political opposition was not responsible for Mussolini's fall on 25 July 1943; it was brought about by the action of the king, and by some elements of the Army and Fascist Party leadership. On 8 September Allied troops landed near Naples; and the new government, led by

1: SS-Oberscharführer, SD, 1943
2: Feldpolizeiassistant, GFP, 1943
3: SS-Brigadeführer u. Gen.Maj. der Polizei, 1943

Norway:
1: Sveitforer, Hird Regt.No.1 'Viken'
2: Overbetjent, Hirdens Bedriftsvern
3: Milorg resistance fighter

Denmark:
1: Schalburgmand, Schalburg Korpset
2: Schalburg-Overvagtmester, Schalburg Korpset
3: Danish resistance fighter

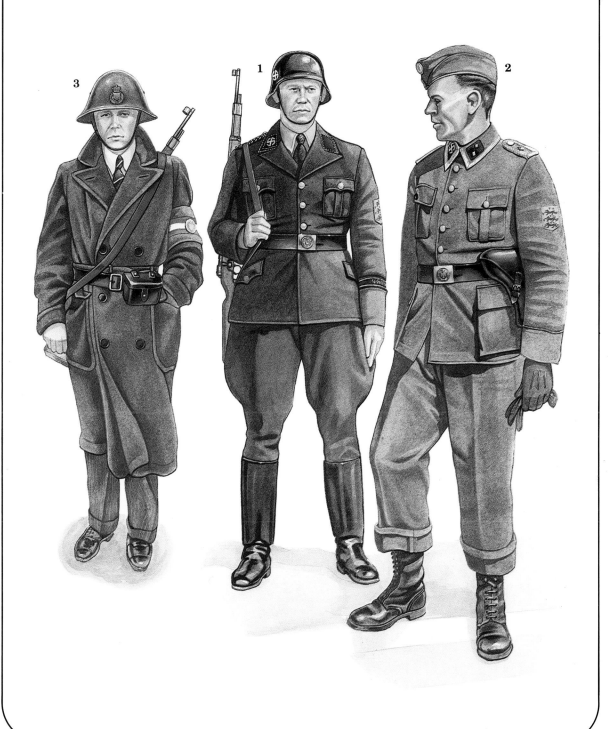

Holland:
1: SS-Hoofdstormleider, Germansche-SS
2: WA-Banleider, Weer Afdeelingen
3: Unterscharführer, Landstorm Nederland, 1944

D

Belgium:
1: Hopman, Dietsche Militie/Zwarte Brigade
2: Onderofficier, Vlaamse Wacht
3: Wachter, Wachtbrigade

E

France:
1: Milicien, Franc Garde Non-Permanente, Milice Francaise
2: Milicien, Corps Francs, Parti Franciste
3: French resistance fighter, 1944

F

Italy and Tyrol:
1: Zugführer, Standschutzen-Btl. 'Meran'
2: Divisional commander, Italian partisans, Ossola Valley
3: Tenente, Guardia Nazionale Repubblicana

G

Italy:
1: Guardiamarina, XªDivisione MAS
2: Colonello, Fanteria, Esercito Repubblicano
3: Commandante di plotone, Brigata Nera 'Aldo Resega'

Marshal Badoglio, announced the armistice which had been negotiated in secret some days before. The king and Badoglio fled Rome; and the anti-Fascist parties—the Socialist, Liberal, Christian Democrat and Communist Parties—created the National Liberation Committee, CLN. The CLN was not recognised in the north of Italy, however, where the Communists had great support, and where their own National Liberation Committee of Upper Italy, CLNAI, was formed. Local sub-committees linked to either the CLN or the CLNAI were formed in all the regions and cities occupied by the Germans. Relations were very bad between the Badoglio government, which was recognised by the Allies, and the Liberation Committees, until the king's abdication and the formation in June 1944 of a new government including members of the CLN.

Meanwhile, Mussolini was freed from detention on the Gran Sasso by Otto Skorzeny's airborne commando raid of 12 September 1943. He established, in the areas occupied by the Germans, the so-called Repubblica Sociale Italiana. While the monarchist government in the south tried to create 'co-belligerent' forces to fight alongside the Allies, the government of the RSI organised its own armed and police forces, which were employed mainly to fight the guerrilla movements sponsored by the CLN and CLNAI. In formal terms the RSI was an Allied country, so no German authority was appointed to hold power over it. However, considering the whole territory as an area of military operations, Germany's military commanders in fact enjoyed a large measure of control. Germany also annexed to the Reich areas of northern Italy which had formerly belonged to the Austrian empire.

The first resistance operations were carried out by the Communists, who created the **Gruppi di Azioni Patriottici**, GAP. During 1944 partisan groups began to be active in rural and mountain areas. The *partigiani* organised themselves in 'brigades', their different titles reflecting different political complexions. The 'Garibaldi' Brigades, the most numerous and active, were made up of Communists. The Socialists raised '**Matteoti**' Brigades; and the '**Giustizia e Liberta**' Brigades were formed by the Social Democrat/Liberal 'Action Party'. Autonomous brigades were also raised by the Christian Democrats and Liberals.

October 1943: recruits to the Italian RSI forces are issued field equipment. The Royal Army insignia have been removed from the uniforms, and (right) the RSI's *gladius* and wreath insignia has been added to the collars. (Rallo)

The RSI forces

The creation of the RSI Armed Forces was attended by political problems. A radical Fascist group led by Ricci pressed for the formation of an openly politicised Fascist Army, to avoid the recurrence of 'treachery' such as that of Badoglio. But the Army officers who remained loyal to Mussolini, led by Marshal Graziani, argued for the formation of non-political armed forces. The solution adopted was a compromise.

Ricci was authorised to raise the **Guardia Nazionale Repubblicana**, GNR; this came into being on 8 December 1943, drawing upon ex-members of the 'Blackshirt' MVSN units of the old Royal Army, Carabinieri, members of the Italian African Police, and young recruits. With a total strength of about 150,000, their main mission was 'the maintenance of order in the rear areas'. The GNR had a number of specialised branches, the so-called 'GNR Speciali':

The **GNR Postelegrafica** (Postal and Telegraph Guard) had 21 detachments termed Reparti.

The **GNR della Montagna e della Foresta** (Mountain and Forestry Guard) comprised a single battalion.

The **GNR Portuaria** (Port Guard) had three detachments.

The **GNR Ferroviaria** (Railway Guard) had nine regiments, termed Legione.

The **GNR di Frontiera** (Frontier Guard) had four regiments.

The **GNR Stradale** (Highway Guard).

The remainder of the GNR formed the **GNR**

The collarless tunic and roll-neck sweater were widely used throughout the RSI forces. This member of the Marine 'San Marco' Division wears the characteristic collar patches. The helmet was often painted with insignia, here unidentifiable. (Rallo)

June 1944, Sennelager training area: Vittorio Mussolini, the Duce's son, in conversation with Gen. Agosti, commander of the RSI's 'Littorio' Division. Mussolini displays a colonel's cap ranking, in the system common to the RSI armed forces, the GNR, XªMAS, etc. Gen. Agosti's uniform seems to be a privately devised outfit; it resembles that of a German general, without the eagle-and-swastika insignia, and with the RSI badge on the collar patches. His cap bears the Italian general officer's eagle with the royal crown removed. (Rallo)

Arma Combattente, comprising: ten regiments; 16 battalions; eight 'storm units' (one legion and seven battalions, normally using the initial M for Mussolini in their titles); an armoured battalion; one parachute battalion; and two anti-tank battalions. The GNR's attempts to form the Anti-Aircraft and Anti-Parachute divisions 'Etna' and 'Vesubio' never reached fruition.

The GNR was not well equipped or organised. The mixture of elements from the MVSN, Carabinieri, and young recruits was far from the 'political army' of which Ricci had dreamed; and the project came to an end in August 1944 when the GNR was incorporated into the RSI Armed Forces.

As defence minister of the RSI, Graziani was responsible for the Army (**Esercito Repubblicano**), Navy (**Marina Militare Repubblicana**) and Air Force (**Aeronautica Nazionale Repubblicana**). The first conscription orders went out in October 1943—a move which indirectly helped the partisans, as many young men fled to the hills rather than be taken for the RSI forces.

The Air Force had several combat squadrons, and also ground units—particularly parachute units such as the 'Folgore' Regt., 'Fulmina' Bn. etc. The Navy had only small vessels, and its main contribution was the Marine units.

The Republican Army had a total strength of some 400,000, and was employed against the Resistance. The order of battle at the time of its peak strength was as follows:

Divisions (each with two infantry and one artillery regiment):
Iª Divisione Bersaglieri 'Italia'
IIª Div. Granatieri 'Littorio'
IIIª Div. Fanteria de Marina 'San Marco'

IVᵃDiv. Alpina 'Monterrosa'

Task forces:
'Cacciatori degli Appenini' Group (two regts., some autonomous bns.)
'Reparti Anti-Partigiani' Group (five bns.)
'Reparti Autonomi Bersaglieri' (two regts.)
Autonomous units:
Armoured Groups 'Leoncello' and 'San Giusto'
Alpine Regt. 'Tagliamento'
Eight coastal artillery groups
Eight bns. and 20 cos. on security and coastal defence duties.

The four divisions were trained in Germany, using German drill, and each had a German staff. They returned to Italy between June and December 1944, but were not sent to the front to fight the Allies; instead they formed the 'Liguria' Army, with the mission of fighting the Resistance, and guarding the coasts against Allied landings behind the Axis front lines.

Other units with a special status included the Italian Waffen-SS Brigade[1]; and the **XᵃMAS**.

The XᵃMAS was originally an MTB flotilla specialising in attacks on British naval bases in the Mediterranean by means of frogmen and 'human torpedoes'; this élite unit, which achieved some notable successes, was commanded by Prince Junio Valerio Borghese. Borghese offered his services to Germany immediately after the Italian-Allied armistice; and his command thereafter enjoyed the status of a kind of 'free corps', independent of the rest of the RSI forces.

Borghese created a 'private army' with a strength of nearly 25,000; it included all branches of the Army as well as Navy units, and was spread out all over RSI territory. In May 1944 the main effectives were grouped together in the so-called XᵃDivisione MAS, comprising:

Two infantry regts. (the first with the 'Barbarigo', 'Lupo' and 'NP' Bns.; the second with the 'Fulmine', 'Sagittario' and 'Valanga' Bns.).

One artillery regt. ('San Giorgio', 'Da Giussano' and 'Colleoni' Groups).

The XᵃDivisione MAS proved to be one of the most effective of the anti-partisan formations.

In July 1944 the **Brigate Nere** ('Black Brigades') were set up, theoretically incorporating

June 1944, Grafenwohr training area; Benito Mussolini speaks to Gen. Farina, commander of the 'San Marco' Division. Note the collarless tunic and sweater; the collar patches with the 'lion of St Mark' above the RSI badge; and the general's eagle badge painted on the helmet. The two generals (left and centre) display ranking only on the shoulder boards, and no longer on the cuffs. (Rallo)

all male members of the Fascist Party. By this date it was evident that the GNR would never be a 'Fascist Party army'; and the Esercito Repubblicano was still training in Germany. In the face of a growing partisan offensive the general secretary of the Fascist Party, Pavolini, ordered the arming and mobilisation of all party members. Each local section (obviously, only in large towns) had to create a para-military unit. Forty territorial Black Brigades were created. There was also a Raggruppamento di Brigate Nere Mobili, comprising six mobile brigades; three Brigate Nere Operative; and minor units such as the 'Onore e Combatimento' Group, the Young Fascists' Company 'Bir el Gubi', etc.

Each brigade was named after a Fascist killed by the Resistance. The strength of these units depended upon the size of the town where it had its

[1]See MAA 34, *The Waffen-SS*, Revised Edition.

headquarters and the number of local party members: some could only field a single company, others a regiment. The total strength of the organisation was about 100,000 men, committed to fighting the partisans.

The police forces must also be mentioned. The **Pubblica Sicurezza** organised special battalions to fight the Resistance; and the Polizia Ausiliaria was raised with the same mission. A special case was the **Legione Autonoma Mobile 'Ettore Muti'**, a very active anti-partisan unit some 4,000 strong, organised in autonomous companies, and even boasting some light armoured cars. Theoretically a police unit answerable to the RSI internal affairs ministry, it was in fact a kind of 'free corps' similar to the XᵃMAS. Its operational area lay in and around Milan.

Uniforms

The uniforms of the RSI Armed Forces and the para-military security units did not follow clear regulations. Initially the monarchist symbols were simply removed from pre-armistice uniforms. At the end of 1944 new regulations were issued; but in practice the situation was chaotic, with new items arriving intermittently, and continued use of clothing and insignia of Royal Army and German origin. Each formation tended to adopt its own style, particularly the XᵃMAS, Legione Muti, and Brigate Nere.

The most common garments were those of the

February 1945, Milan: Pavolini, General Secretary of the Fascist Party, inspects the Black Brigade 'Aldo Resega'. The black shirt and mountain cap worn with the grey-green tunic and trousers was the most popular uniform among the Black Brigades at this date. Compare with Plate H3.

parachutist's uniform introduced in 1941, particularly the collarless tunic. Generally the grey-green uniform colour was retained, though there was much use of the Navy dark blue or the black roll-neck sweater. In place of the crown and five-pointed star symbols of the Royal forces, the RSI adopted as the general Armed Forces badge a Roman *gladius* (short sword) within a laurel wreath. The use of the traditional pointed collar patches or 'flames' was continued, though new rectangular ones were also issued, and sometimes both shapes were combined—'flames' rising from a squared-off base. The Marine units (the XᵃMAS, and the 'San Marco' Division under Army command) used collar patches recalling the shape of a shoulder strap, being squared at the base but rising to a triangular point. Some other small units used similar patches.

Although rank badges were different for the Army, Navy, GNR etc., in practice all RSI military forces adopted a common ranking system for use on the field caps—the traditional Italian forage cap, the beret, and the newly introduced mountain cap similar to the German pattern. This ranking system was almost identical to that previously used by the Royal Army.

In the Republican Army rank badges were removed from the cuff. Ranking was displayed on the shoulder straps by officers and senior NCOs, and on the sleeves by junior ranks. The fighting arms used the three-point collar patch (infantry, artillery, etc.); the non-combatant services (medical, ordnance, etc.) used single-point patches. All bore the RSI sword-and-laurels emblem in silver. The patch could be either in a single colour (e.g. red for infantry, green for Alpini, etc.), or in a combination of colours (e.g. yellow-orange background edged with green for mountain artillery). Each arm or service had its own cap badge.

As can be seen in the accompanying photos and colour plates, the Marine units wore very distinctive collar patches. The 'San Marco' Division wore red collar patches bearing the silver RSI emblem and a small gold 'lion of St Mark'; this formation used Army rank badges. The XᵃDivisione MAS collar patches changed from red to blue in July 1944, with the same devices as the 'San Marco'; but Navy-style ranking was retained, and a formation arm shield was worn. The autonomous units of Prince

July 1944: paratroopers of the 'Folgore' Regt., now an élite unit of the RSI Air Force, salute with their daggers; they wear the camouflage smock and special padded helmet used by Royal Army paratroopers pre-1943. (Neulen)

Borghese's 'private army' displayed many different badges and shields.

The GNR Arma Combattente wore two-point black collar patches; the GNR Speciali the same but with coloured edges. The RSI emblem was usually worn on the patches, but other symbols included a silver double-M shaped like a lightning bolt; a yellowish *fascio*; and a red M combined with a silver *fascio*. Ranking was worn on the cuffs by officers, on the shoulder straps by NCOs, and on the sleeves by other ranks. The GNR Arma Combattente had a cap badge in the shape of a *fascio* between two stylised wings; the GNR Speciali each had different cap badges.

The Brigate Nere used black shirts as their main uniform garment, with grey-green tunics and trousers, or civilian clothes. Each brigade had a small rectangular red and black patch, bearing the name of the unit, above the left breast pocket. Initially rank was shown by means of a system of coloured lanyards; in 1945 GNR ranks and rank badges were introduced. Not all the Black Brigades wore collar patches, but in general they used a three-pointed black 'flame' on a red squared-off base; other colours were possible, e.g. green for the Alpine brigades. The Black Brigades' red *fascio*

badge appeared on the collar patches, and on the black mountain cap adopted by this organisation. Other widely seen cap badges were a silver skull with a sword between the teeth, and the SS skull.

The Publica Sicurezza units continued to wear traditional police uniforms, but with a new cap badge similar to that of the Italian SS units. A silver skull or *fascio* was worn on their rectangular, crimson collar patches. The Legione Muti wore grey-green uniforms with collar patches shaped like those of the Marines, but in black, and bearing a red *fascio* and a silver skull.

The Partisans

The Resistance was able to raise a large number of armed units—an authentic army—in the German rear areas. They adopted classic military designations, with 'divisions', 'brigades' and 'battalions'; but in fact these units were much smaller than their titles suggested—a battalion had 30 men, a brigade 100, and a division 300–400. The partisan officers were recognised as such by the Allies in

The GNR Armoured Group 'Leonessa' wore a copy of German *Panzer* uniform in black. The large beret, in imitation of the German *Schutzmütze*, bears what seems to be a cloth death's-head badge; the collar device is a red 'M' for Mussolini, with a silver *fascio*. (Neulen)

1945; divisional commanders were given the rank of major, brigade commanders were appointed captain, and battalion commanders were made lieutenants.

The Resistance effort increased steadily during the first half of 1944. The fall of Cassino and the liberation of Rome in June 1944 allowed the Allies to advance more swiftly; and in August, at Florence, the partisans took a direct part in a battle in support of the Allies for the first time.

During that summer the CLNAI ordered the creation of 'free areas'; and between June and December 1944 15 small 'partisan republics' were established in such areas as the Langhe, the Ossola Valley close to the Swiss border, Montferrato, etc. The existence of these 'republics' was ephemeral— some lasted six weeks, others four months; but that they could be established at all was a proof of the strength and confidence of the partisans, and large Wehrmacht and RSI forces had to be assembled to wipe them out.

From June 1944 the military formations of the Resistance grouped themselves under the name **Corpo di Volontari della Libertà**, CVL; the high command included Gen. Cardona, and the Communist Luigi Longo.

The end of 1944 brought an adverse change in the balance of forces. The GNR had proved itself unable to eradicate the partisans; but the return from Germany of the RSI divisions, the establishment of the Black Brigades, and the setting up of the XᵃDivisione MAS created new dangers for the

Resistance. They also suffered a severe psychological blow in November 1944, when the Supreme Allied Commander in Italy, Field Marshal Alexander, ordered the CVL to scale down its operations and adopt a defensive posture, at the same time cutting down their vital logistic support. The ostensible reason was the impossibility of maintaining the Allied advance that winter, as the British and US troops were tied down in front of the formidable Gothic Line defences. Some have suggested that the growing power of the Communist partisans was also regarded as undesirable. It was at this time that the German and RSI authorities were able to do the Resistance serious damage by the arrest of many high-ranking CLNAI and CVL officers. In order to survive the harsh winter, many partisans left the mountains and took refuge in towns.

In spring 1945 the Resistance went back on to the offensive with vigour. In the days before the German surrender in Italy there were major partisan risings in important towns in industrial northern Italy: in Genova on 23 April, in Milan on 24 April, and in Torino on 25 April.

On 15 April 1945 the CVL order of battle represented formidable forces. Taking the brigade as the most typical unit (either within a partisan division, or operating independently), there were 357 Communist brigades; 50 Socialist brigades; 191 'Giustizia e Libertà' brigades, and 87 Liberal and Christian Democrat autonomous brigades. In Lombardy alone 26 divisions were active, together with 25 independent brigades and 15 other independent groups. The guerrilla effectives must be put at around 250,000 men, although at the end of the war these figures increased with the rapid enlistment of many opportunists.

Partisan uniforms, generally, did not exist, except for some adopted by formations in the Ossola Valley area—see Plate G2. Usually the guerrillas wore civilian clothes or garments of Italian armed forces or Wehrmacht origin. The 'Garibaldini' of the Communist units wore large red neck-scarves. The CVL adopted its own rank system, displayed on small patches above the left breast pocket; but the 'Garibaldi' units continued to use systems of their own, which always featured the red star emblem.

The guerrilla warfare in Italy was more ferocious

Partisans from the Ossola Valley, in their home-made dark brown wool uniforms with Alpine hats and edelweiss collar patches—see Plate G2.

than in any other Western European country. Both sides killed large numbers of their enemies. The Communists were the first to use terror methods; and the Germans, predictably, responded by taking indiscriminate reprisals which only increased the hatred in which they were held. In no other country was it so obvious that a civil war was being fought; the Communists killed not only the Fascists, but any other anti-Communists, and there were large-scale armed confrontations between partisan groups of different political allegiances.

When the war ended the north of Italy saw a wave of savage reprisals against those who had supported Mussolini. In this dreadful final chapter to a short but extremely fierce guerrilla war, some 100,000 people lost their lives.

The Plates

A1: SS-Oberscharführer, Sicherheitsdienst, 1943

It was unusual for SD personnel to turn out in full combat equipment, of which they seem to have had limited and out of date supplies for their essentially second-line duties: their victims, after all, could seldom fight back. . . . This senior NCO's appearance still reflects the policeman more than the soldier. He wears the 1937 all-grey SS tunic, with its collar pressed open over a shirt collar and tie—a common practice among SD NCOs, who normally wore a white rather than the brown SS shirt. The breeches are in the slightly contrasting 'new grey' shade. His right-hand collar patch is the blank black type identifying the SD; conventional SS ranking is worn on the left patch. Photos show NCO tunics worn both closed and open, both with and without conventional NCO Tresse braid. The SS arm eagle, with its distinctive pointed wings, is worn on the left upper sleeve; the silver-grey on black 'SD' diamond patch on the left forearm. Pre-1942, conventional SS shoulder straps were worn, with 'toxic green' Waffenfarbe. Thereafter these Police-style straps were introduced, in interwoven black and silver cord with green underlay. The outdated MP28 was widely used by the SS and SD.

A2: Feldpolizeiassistant, Geheime Feldpolizei, 1943

When in uniform this Secret Field Police investigator wears the unremarkable service dress of an Army NCO, apart from certain peculiarities of insignia. All members of the GFP were in fact Wehrmachtbeamten or 'armed forces officials', not full members of the Army; they were specialists, given uniform and rank in order to allow them to work in their speciality for the armed forces, but only for that purpose. The branch-of-service colour or Waffenfarbe for all Beamten was dark green; this was combined in their insignia with a second colour, Nebenfarbe, identifying the particular organisation. This Feldpolizeiassistant—the rank held by all GFP NCOs—wears pale blue edging on three sides of dark green collar patches bearing conventional silver-grey Litzen. Note that the Army NCO's silver Tresse braid does not appear round the edges of the collar itself. The shoulder straps are of a design entirely unlike normal Army practice, with interwoven pale blue and dark green cords on a pale blue underlay edged dark green, and the 'GFP' monogram in silver for an NCO. Breast and field cap insignia are conventional. The silver-grey on black 'Geheime Feldpolizei' script cuff title was rarely seen.

A3: SS-Brigadeführer und Generalmajor der Polizei, 1943

By this stage of the war a Police General would display in his uniform the close relationship which existed between the Police and the SS, both of them under the supreme command of Heinrich Himmler as Reichsführer-SS und Chef der Deutsche Polizei. On the service cap, in 'Police green' and dark brown, the gold furniture (including the national eagle and swastika in its Police form) are indication of general officer's rank, which is also marked by the wide Lampassen on the breeches. The piped service tunic of the Police, in green with dark brown collar and cuffs and bright green piping, still bears a Police arm eagle; but the collar patches are of the type introduced by Himmler in late 1942 for Police generals—SS rank insignia, in gold on green. The shoulder straps are of the same design as those of a Wehrmacht major-general, but on green underlay. The Siegrunen insignia on the left breast marks full personal membership of the SS.

B1: Sveitfører, Norwegian Hird Regt. No. 1 'Viken'

The basic Hird uniform was a dark blue cap, tunic and trousers; straight trousers and ankle boots were seen more often than these breeches and riding boots. All ranks wore the Sam Browne belt; although trained with small arms, Hird personnel rarely went armed. Some photos suggest that the Hird brassard may have borne metallic braid edging in some cases. The rank—equivalent to captain—is indicated on the shoulder straps; the

Hird differed from most other pro-German militias in not copying the German ranking system. Field ranks wore a gold cap cord. His unit is identified by the 'VIKEN' cuff title of this central Oslo regiment. Another known pattern is 'VIKING', edged in gold braid, and worn by Regt. No.7 from the greater Oslo area. In summer the uniform could be worn without the tunic; in winter, with a dark blue greatcoat. Some photos show an earlier pattern of double-breasted tunic.

B2: Overbetjent, Norwegian Hirdens Bedriftsvern

A senior NCO of the 'Hird Factory Guard', the only permanently barracked unit of the Hird, largely recruited from Eastern Front veterans of the Norwegian Legion. On his field grey uniform this man displays the ribbon of the Iron Cross 2nd Class,

The funeral of a Dutch collaborator killed by the Resistance. In the foreground, two WA men—note scarlet collar patches on black uniforms, cf. Plate D2. In the background, Dutch volunteers in the German NSKK still wear the black breeches of the WA motorised branch with their NSKK tunics and collar patches. Note the 'wolf hook' rune worn as a helmet decal by both organisations. (Neulen)

a German wound badge, and on the left breast the Norwegian Front Fighter badge instituted by Quisling; he also retains his old Waffen-SS belt. The insignia of the HBV resembled those of the Quisling police rather than the Hird itself. The shoulder straps, obviously German-inspired, are of police pattern. The lion and axe emblems on the collar patches, facing inwards, were worn on green patches by the police, on black by the HBV. The cuff title bearing the name of this organisation is the only specific sign of the HBV's Hird affiliation.

B3: Norwegian Milorg resistance fighter, 1945
The use of civilian clothing was, of course, the norm in all the clandestine resistance movements in occupied Europe. Only in 1944–45, when the Germans were retreating or surrendering, did resisters wear openly the brassards of their groups,

usually in simple national colours. The weapon is the British Sten SMG, dropped in its thousands to European resistance movements: it was light, sturdy, easy to use (at short range), easy to conceal, and so simple that any competent local metal shop could repair it.

C1: Schalburgmand, Danish Schalburg Korpset
This private of the Danish branch of the Germanic SS wears the Schalburg Korpset's original uniform, scarcely differing from that of the Allgemeine-SS apart from national insignia. Note the Danish arm shield, different from the simpler type worn by the

Dutch Germanic SS-men parade in all-black uniforms closely modelled on those of the German Allgemeine-SS. Note black-and-silver piping on collar patches and SS-rune right sleeve diamond; 'wolf hook' upper cap badge with transverse bars; and regimental number '3' on right collar patches. See Plate D1.

Vlaamse Fabriekswacht **musicians. Note the new SS-style collar patches, introduced throughout the** *Dietsche Militie.* **The left-hand man displays the left arm shield of the DM—a black 'wolf hook' on an orange-yellow background. The cuff title bears the Gothic letters 'VFW' each side of the triangle-in-a-circle VNV badge. (Centre de Recherches et d'Etudes de la SGM)**

Danish Waffen-SS Freikorps: a yellow shield bearing Denmark's traditional arms of three blue lions and nine red hearts. Cuff titles were worn at company level: this 'Schalburg' title was worn by the Corps staff, NCO School and Guard Company, and others were e.g. 'Herluf Trolle', 'Absalon', etc. Instead of SS runes the collar patch bears a 'mobile' swastika, repeated on the belt buckle, and worn as a cap badge and helmet decal. It was worn on the cap crown with a white surround and stylised wings; below it, the SS death's-head. As in other Germanic SS branches, the collar patches were edged in black and silver twist for enlisted ranks and in silver for officers.

C2: Schalburg-Overvagtmester, Danish Schalburg Korpset
A senior NCO equivalent to SS-Oberscharführer, wearing the more practical uniform used for military duties and based on the Danish Army's 1923 khaki uniform. The trousers turned up over the boots are a characteristically Danish feature. Ranks in the Schalburg Korpset were of police, rather than SS origin, but insignia recall SS

ranking. Note that on the khaki uniform the collar patches did not have cord edging; NCO Tresse braid edged the collar, where appropriate; and the shoulder cord of the black uniform was replaced by two cloth shoulder straps in uniform khaki. Officers wore an open-neck tunic over a white shirt collar and black tie.

C3: Danish resistance fighter, 1945
The resistance movements took over military and security duties in Denmark in the interval between the German surrender and the arrival of British troops. Civilian clothing could thus be embellished openly with bits and pieces of military equipment—here, the Danish steel helmet, and a Danish Army pouch for ammunition for the German Mauser 98K rifle—as well as the brassard in national colours bearing a Danish heraldic shield.

D1: SS-Hoofdstormleider, Dutch Germansche-SS
This officer, of a rank equivalent to SS-Hauptsturmführer, wears a uniform almost identical to that of the Allgemeine-SS. The black shirt, the belt, the left sleeve badge, and the 'wolf hook' worn as the upper cap badge are the distinctively Dutch features. All Dutch SS-men wore this plain black cuff band with silver edges, and the Siegrunen on a black right sleeve diamond, edged in silver for officers. (The latter insignia was also worn by the Norwegian Germanic SS, and on the left sleeve by the Flemish Germanic SS. The Flemish wore a diamond-shaped swastika as the upper cap badge; the Norwegian branch did not wear the service

Vlaamse Wacht **on parade; at left, an officer. Note the Dutch Army helmets, and the small Flemish shield worn on the forearms. (Centre de Recherches et d'Etudes de la SGM)**

dress cap.) The shoulder strap follows Allgemeine-SS practice exactly: silver and black cord for enlisted ranks, plain silver cord for company officers, braided silver cord for field officers. The collar patches show, on his right, the number of his regiment (there were six in all) and his rank on the left. The Dutch SS retained the black uniform throughout their existence, unlike the Norwegians and Flemish, who at first wore transitional styles, and the Danish, who subsequently adopted khaki.

D2: WA-Banleider, Dutch Weer Afdeelingen

Black was the predominant uniform colour throughout the Dutch collaborationist militias and security forces, worn by the Dutch Germanic SS, the WA militia of the NSB, and the 'Communal Police'. The WA ranking system followed that of the SS closely: apart from the red and gold colours, this major wears SS-Sturmbannführer's insignia. The shoulder cords, too, resemble the SS type, though in gold, and worn on both shoulders. On the left sleeve is the black and red triangular patch bearing the 'wolf hook', used by all NSB organisations; note, however, that the 'hook' is yellow, rather than white as in the Dutch SS. This major wears the WA Old Fighter's Medal, and the ribbon of the Iron Cross 2nd Class.

Cap crown and band piping differed with rank. Non-commissioned personnel wore red; junior officers, red and gold mixed; and senior officers, all gold. The upper cap badge, a Dutch heraldic lion holding a sword and a bundle of arrows, was peculiar to officers; other ranks more usually wore a forage cap, in any case.

The Communal Police uniform was similar, though worn with a closed collar. Ranking was in the form of white stars and bars on a blue background. On the cap the police wore a Dutch cockade surrounded by oakleaves on the band, in place of the NSB triangular badge; and a flaming grenade in place of the heraldic lion.

D3: Unterscharführer, Dutch Landstorm Nederland, 1944

There are few photographs of this unit, but we take this figure from one of them.

Initially most members of the Landwacht and Landstorm continued to wear the black uniforms of their parent organisations—the Germanic SS, WA and Communal Police. Field grey uniforms were

Joseph Darnand, Vichy's 'Secretary General for the Maintenance of Order', greets an officer of the GMR. The officer wears a black uniform with light blue collar patches; light blue cuff patches with silver rank insignia; and light blue breeches stripes. A unit badge is worn on the right breast pocket.

introduced progressively. The use of the flaming grenade—doubtless an inheritance from the police—on the collar patch is not surprising, given the wide variety of national collar patch symbols in the Waffen-SS. Its substitution for the death's-head cap badge is more surprising, and in fact unique among Waffen-SS units. The absence of NCO Tresse on the collar may perhaps be explained by the large police element in the German and Dutch cadre of this unit—Tresse was not worn by police NCOs. It is believed that from September 1944 the SS-runes and/or perhaps the 'wolf hook' may have replaced the grenade on the collar patches, marking the unit's full incorporation into the Waffen-SS. According to some sources the unit wore on the left sleeve, below the SS eagle, a patch in the form of the word 'Landwacht' above a Dutch heraldic lion

Milicien **escorting the coffin of a collaborator killed by the Resistance; the pall-bearers wear the blue shirts of one of the French Fascist parties.**

right patch displayed the unit number (here 'IV' and '18'), and the left the rank; as in the SS, senior officers wore ranking on both patches.

The arm badge remained unchanged from 1940 to 1945. The Tollenaere Badge, incorporating the 'wolf hook', was awarded to VNV 'old fighters' and to Eastern Front veterans. Non-commissioned ranks usually wore forage caps. When operating as Hilfsgendarmerie in support of the German authorities, ZB men wore the German brassard 'In the service of the German Armed Forces'.

E2: Onderofficier, Flemish Vlaamse Wacht
The VW at first wore Belgian uniforms, and in 1944 they were issued field grey; but for much of the war they used this midnight blue uniform, with yellow piping. (The parallel Garde Wallone used the same uniform with red distinctives, and Belgian steel helmets when necessary.)

The battalion number—here, 'II'—is displayed in Roman numerals in a wreath on the breast and cap. Rank was initially shown by white stripes on the cuffs for NCOs, and 'pips' on the collar patches for officers. Later, ranking was limited to the shoulder straps, and all ranks wore these plain black collar patches piped in yellow. This NCO wears German-style Tresse on his collar and shoulder straps. According to duties, the VW wore steel helmets (of Dutch, and very rarely of German pattern), and carried small arms and rifle equipment.

E3: Wachter, Flemish Wachtbrigade
The uniforms of this Flemish organisation recruited by the Luftwaffe evolved steadily, as its designation changed from Fabriekswacht (FW or VFW), through Wachtbrigade, and finally to the Flemish Flak Brigade. The Fabriekswacht wore the same uniform as the Black Brigade, but with a cuff title on which the Gothic letters 'VFW' were repeated twice; their cap badge was distinctive, being a seamew shaped strikingly like the Luftwaffe's eagle. Like the Black Brigade, the retitled Wachtbrigade (WB or VWB) adopted a rank system following the SS model, with stripes and 'pips' on green rectangular collar patches.

Always under the command of the German military authorities, this organisation received small arms and field equipment (including the

supported by laurel sprays. No photographic evidence for the use of this insignia, which supposedly disappeared from October 1943, has been found by the present author. There were several slightly different versions of a 'Landwacht' cuff title; and one lettered 'Landstorm Nederland' has been described.

This figure would wear the German 1943 field grey trousers, canvas anklets, and ankle boots. Again, sources unsupported by photographic evidence describe decals for the German helmet in the form of a Dutch tricolour shield bearing the heraldic lion, and a flaming grenade.

E1: Hopman, Flemish Dietsche Militie/Zwarte Brigade
The 'Black Brigade' was the main branch of the Flemish collaborationist DM militia; like their Dutch counterparts, they favoured black uniforms and the 'wolf hook' rune, which appeared on the cap, the arm shield, and—surrounded by the legend 'Recht en Trouw'—on the belt buckle.

The black is relieved only by the green of the collar patches and shoulder straps. These went through several changes over the years. Initially the patches were shaped rather like Italian 'flame' patches; officers displayed rank insignia on them, while enlisted ranks wore ranking on the shoulder straps. Subsequently, new patches and straps clearly inspired by the SS type replaced these. The

Luftwaffe helmet) earlier than other collaborationist militias and auxiliaries. Like the Flemish volunteers serving in the Waffen-SS, they wore a cuff shield in yellow with a black lion emblem; initially the FW had worn the same arm insignia as the Black Brigade. The belt buckle also bears the Flemish shield device, surrounded by oakleaves and the legend 'Het Vaderland Getrouwe'.

F1: Milicien, Franc Garde Non-Permanente, Milice Française

When the SOL was re-organised and retitled 'Milice Française' in January 1943, they received new uniforms: dark blue tunics, trousers and berets, and khaki shirts. The Greek letter *gamma* was adopted as the emblem of the organisation, and appeared on the beret, tunic, blue greatcoat and black-painted Adrian helmet. A rank system was developed, and displayed on the shoulder straps; and unit numbers were worn on the collar patches. In summer shirtsleeve uniform was worn, with a *gamma* brassard. The accompanying photos show this uniform.

The Franc Garde Non-Permanente were a part-time element, serving only a few hours on a few days weekly, or upon general mobilisation. Their uniforms were a good deal less regular: this unprepossessing character, partly based upon a well-known photograph, has no collar patches, and wears an aggressively civilian shirt. His decorations would seem to identify him as a veteran of both the First World War and the Russian Front in the Second.

F2: Milicien, Corps Francs, Parti Françiste

Most French Fascist party militias wore blue shirts, and those of the Parti Françiste militia were the lightest shade. The Corps Francs militiamen had black shoulder straps, displaying a ranking system which the present author has as yet been unable to identify. The party leader, Bucard, had a bodyguard known as the Main Bleu ('Blue Hand') who also wore black collars and cuffs. Theoretically, the shirts were worn with navy blue trousers and ties, but photos show a wide range of other civilian colours. The party badge was worn on the right breast: it combined the motifs of a cog wheel, an ear of barley, and the Vichy double-bladed axe emblem. Like other French Fascist political militias, the Corps Francs acquired small arms for use in clashes with the Resistance.

F3: French resistance fighter, 1944

For reasons which are touched upon in the text, the French resistance groups saw more open fighting against German troops than their Dutch, Belgian and Scandinavian counterparts. As the Germans fell back across France in the face of the Allied invasion, the Resistance attacked convoys, encircled isolated garrisons, and helped liberate many towns. They usually wore civilian clothing, with various kinds of brassard; although large groups in rural areas frequently adopted the French Army rank system, and such odd items of 1940 uniform as they had to hand. Weapons were mainly of British origin, air-dropped through the auspices of SOE;

A proud member of the Breton resistance, which actively helped the advance of Allied troops in 1944, poses by a relic of occupation. He wears an American helmet, and on the sleeve of his civilian jacket a brassard bearing the word '*Milice*' or '*Police*'.

March 1945: Benito Mussolini inspects the *Brigata Nera Mobile Alpina 'Leonessa'* **('Alpine Mobile Black Brigade "Lioness"').
These men wear** *Alpini*-**style hats; and the officer at right shows clearly the double-pointed green 'flame' of Alpine troops worn on a new black backing patch—the small added insignia is the red** *fascio* **of the Black Brigades. (Neulen)**

cached French types; or captured German weapons. Small arms were plentiful; light machine guns like this Bren less so, and much prized, since they allowed attacks from slightly less suicidally close ranges, and had the hitting-power to knock out softskin vehicles. This *maquisard* carries spare magazines in an old French Army gasmask haversack.

G1: *Zugführer, South Tyrolean Standschutzen-Bataillon 'Meran'*

These battalions, raised among ethnic Germans in the South Tyrol/northern Italy border area, were static defence units of the Volkssturm. This figure belongs to the unit raised around Merano, to give it its Italian name. A motley collection of uniform and equipment was issued, including Army tunics without shoulder straps, Police steel helmets, etc. They were authorised to wear the Alpine troops'

edelweiss badge on the German mountain cap. Although there are few photographs, one does show the arm badge of this unit clearly: a green diamond piped in yellow, bearing the Tyrolean eagle in red, above the unit title in light green. Some sources state that these units used Volkssturm collar patches; but in a letter to the author David Littlejohn states that the patches were in green, rather than black, as the units were raised by the Police rather than the Party.

G2: *Divisional Commander, Italian partisans, Ossola Valley, 1944*

The Italian partisans, under their co-ordinating CVL, were the only Resistance in Western Europe to establish their own complete system of ranks and insignia. These were in the form of silver stars and bars on red or green backgrounds, worn on the left breast. The Communist 'Garibaldi' units also had their own rank insignia, in which the red star figured prominently. The red scarf, universal among Communist partisans, was also worn by some non-Communists. Most partisans wore civilian clothing, or odds and ends of Italian and

German uniform. Only the Ossola Valley units near the Swiss border produced their own uniform: an Alpini-style hat, tunic and trousers in brown, with the scarf worn in this distinctive way under the shoulder straps, and green collar patches bearing a white edelweiss. This commander of a 'division' (in practice, a weak battalion) wears three silver stars and a bar on a red background; the divisional commissar would wear the same but on green backing. He wears an Italian Army officer's belt and is armed with a P38 pistol and Beretta M1938A sub-machine gun.

G3: Tenente, Italian Guardia Nazionale Repubblicana, 1944

As in other formations raised by the RSI, the grey-green collarless 'parachutist' tunic and baggy trousers worn with laced boots were widely seen in the GNR. The new mountain cap bears the GNR badge of a *fascio* with stylised wings; officers wore this, and the chin cord, in gold, while the enlisted ranks wore silver badges. Officers' ranking was worn on the cuffs; senior NCOs', on the shoulder straps; and other ranks, on the sleeves. There were a variety of collar patch designs, but this 'double-M' on black 'flames' was the most widely employed. (Rank insignia, collar patches, and the black shirts worn by GNR personnel all owed their design to the MVSN Fascist Militia units within the Royal Army between 1923 and 1943.) Apart from the mountain cap, the GNR also wore black berets, and the Alpini hat.

H1: Guardiamarina, Italian Xª Divisione MAS, 1944

The uniforms of the XªMAS were of Army design, with Navy ranks and insignia. The distinctive collar patches were originally red; after the formation of the 'San Marco' Division they were changed to light blue, with the exception of the 'Barbarigo' Bn.—this unit, which fought the Allied troops at Anzio, retained the red patches. The devices are the 'lion of St Mark' and the RSI's national badge of a shortsword and laurels. The helmet bears the rank device of the Guardiamarina; an 'X' or an anchor device was sometimes seen in this position. The arm shield originated in that of the XªFlottiglia Motoscafo Anti-Sommergibile—'10th Anti-Sub-marine Motorboat Flotilla'—Prince Borghese's old unit. The skull and rose emblem and Roman

Guerrillas of an Italian Communist 'Garibaldi' brigade; the only 'uniform' items are red scarves—note how they are worn under the shoulder straps. The left breast rank insignia are different from the standardised CVL type, consisting of red bars on a black backing. The red stars above the ranking are on a white circular backing, and have a green disc in the centre—together displaying the Italian national colours.

numeral were retained, the wording simply being changed to 'Divisione'. The Navy's roll neck sweater was widely adopted throughout the RSI Armed Forces.

H2: Colonello, Fanteria, Italian Esercito Repubblicano, 1944

In essentials, this infantry colonel's uniform has hardly changed since the Royal Army prior to the armistice of 1943. Ranking still appears on the shoulder boards but not now on the cuffs. The new RSI national badge appears on the collar patches; and the infantry branch badge worn on the forage cap has lost its crown. The rank continues to be displayed on the left side of the cap. The red of the infantry is worn on the collar patches, the shoulder board piping, and as piping between the two black officers' stripes on the breeches. These latter are in the 'mouse grey' of officers' uniforms pre-1943; the shades of the photo from which we take this figure suggest that tunic and cap are in the 'grey-green' previously used for other ranks' uniforms.

H3: Comandante di plotone, Italian Brigate Nere, 1944

There was much variety in the exact appearance of

these units. The red *fascio* of the Black Brigades was worn on the common black mountain cap; and the unit title on a red and black patch on the left breast—here, 'Aldo Resega'. Initially the only rank insignia were coloured lanyards, the silver and red type illustrated being the mark of a 'platoon commander', equivalent to lieutenant. Progressively the Brigades received the grey-green tunic, and collar patches started to be displayed, bearing the red *fascio*. At the end of the war GNR rank badges were being worn on the tunic and on the black shirt.

Notes sur les planches en couleur

A1 Les sous-officiers de cette organisation portaient souvent des uniformes reflétant une affiliation à la Police plutôt qu'à la *Wehrmacht*—par exemple, des tuniques de qualité pour officiers portées avec un col ouvert sur la chemise et une cravate, des pantalons et des bottes de cavalerie, etc. L'équipement de combat présenté ici est typique—il était rarement porté et souvent d'un modèle démodé. **A2** Noter les insignes de col et d'épaules dans le style de *Wehrmachtbeamten*, comprenant à la fois la couleur bleu pâle identifiant le *GFP* et le vert foncé porté par tous les *Beamten*. Le brassard n'était pas très porté. **A3** A dater du début de 1943, les généraux de la Police ont abandonné les insignes de col *Litzen* et ont porté une version or-sur-vert des insignes de grade des généraux SS. Le *Sigrunen* SS indique l'appartenance personnelle au corps des SS.

B1 Les pantalons et les bottes de cavalerie étaient moins communs que les pantalons droits et des bottines. Le grade—il s'agit ici d'un capitaine—est indiqué sur les épaulettes; le cordon de coiffe indique un officier. Le brassard identifie le Régiment 'Viken' du centre d'Oslo. **B2** De nombreuses caractéristiques allemandes sont portées par cette unité, seule unité en caserne de la BDV, recrutée parmi les SS vétérans de Russie. **B3** Le brassard était évidemment le seul signe d'organisation militaire porté par ce groupe clandestin et seulement en 1945.

C1 L'uniforme précoce était presque identique à l'uniforme allemand de Allgemeine-SS, sauf les insignes nationales sur la coiffe, le col et la manche. Le brassard permet de reconnaître la compagnie—ici la compagnie des Gardes. **C2** Uniforme militaire plus pratique, basé sur la tenue de l'armée danoise de 1923. **C3** A l'époque de la libération, certains articles de l'armée danoise étaient portés ouvertement par la Résistance.

D1 Ce capitaine porte un uniforme virtuellement identique à celui de son homologue allemand, sauf la chemise noire, les insignes de bras, l'insigne de coiffe supérieur et l'insigne de col indiquant son immatriculation régimentale. Toutes les unités hollandaises portaient le brassard uni. **D2** Sur la base des styles SS, l'uniforme WA avait des insignes rouges de col et la couleur du liséré de coiffe différait avec le rang—il s'agit ici d'un major. L'insigne triangulaire est celui du NSB. **D3** Nous avons copié une des rares photographies de cette unité qui existent encore. L'insigne à grenade rappelle celui de la Communal Police, parmi laquelle certains soldats étaient recrutés.

E1 Tout comme les groupes de collaborateurs hollandais, la Brigade Noire portait des uniformes noirs et la rune 'croc de loup' en insigne. Initialement, les insignes de col verts avaient des formes comme les 'flammes' italiennes, ils furent ultérieurement remplacés par des versions ressemblant aux insignes SS. **E2** Noter le numéro de bataillon sur la poitrine et la coiffe; insignes de grades sur les épaulettes et insignes de col unis pour tous les grades; *tresse* de style allemand sur le col et les épaulettes. Les *Garde Wallonne* portaient le même uniforme mais avec des lisérés rouge. **E3** Cette organisation, levée et équipée par la Luftwaffe, présentait des styles WA, Luftwaffe et SS dans son uniforme final.

F1 Noter l'absence d'épaulettes et d'insignes de grade et la chemise de civil portés par ce milicien à temps partiel; et un mélange de décorations françaises et allemandes—c'était probablement un vétéran de la LVF. **F2** Une des nombreuses milices du parti fasciste français, dont la plupart portaient des chemises bleues. **F3** *Maquisard* de 1944, durant les combats intensifs accompagnant les débarquements des alliés.

G1 Faisant partie de la Volkssturm, ces bataillons du Tyrol portaient des insignes de col verts car ils étaient recrutés par la Police. Noter l'insigne de bras et l'absence d'épaulettes. **G2** Le seul groupe de partisans qui porta un uniforme complet; noter les insignes de col *edelweiss* et les insignes de grade du type CVL standard. **G3** Une des conceptions les plus communes de plusieurs types d'insignes de col portés par les hommes de GNR; la tunique sans col et les pantalons larges étaient très populaires dans les forces RSI. Des bérets et des chapeaux alpins étaient portées à côté de cette casquette.

H1 Uniforme de type armée; insignes de grade de type marine, insignes de col ressemblant à ceux des fusiliers marins et insignes de manche inspirés par ceux de l'ancienne flotille de torpilleurs motorisés du Prince Borghese. **H2** Peu de différences par rapport à l'uniforme précédent de l'Armée Royale, à part la disparition de la couronne sur tous les insignes, l'adoption de l'insigne de col à épée-dans-guirlande de la RSI et l'absence d'insignes de grade sur les manchettes. **H3** Insignes de brigade sur le sein gauche; grade indiqué par cordon sur l'épaule.

Farbtafeln

A1 Die Unteroffiziere dieser Organisation trugen häufig Uniformen, die eher an die Polizei als an die *Wehrmacht* erinnerten, beispielsweise Offiziersjacken mit offenem Kragen über Hemd und Krawatte, Kniehosen und Reitstiefel usw. Die hier gezeigte Feldausrüstung ist typisch; sie wurde selten getragen und hatte oft ein altmodisches Muster. **A2** Man beachte die Kragen- und Schulterstreifen im Stil der *Wehrmachtsbeamten* mit der hellblauen Farbe GFP und dem Dunkelgrün der *Beamten*. Der Ärmelstreif wurde nur selten getragen. **A3** Ab Frühjahr 1943 ersetzten die Polizeigenerale die *Litzen*-Kragenabzeichen durch eine golden-grüne Version von Rangabzeichen der SS Generale. Die *Siegrunen* der SS weisen ein Mitglied dieser Organisation aus.

B1 Kniehosen und Reitstiefel waren weniger verbreitet als Hosen und kurze Stiefel. Der Rang (in diesem Fall ein Hauptmann) wurde durch Schulterstreifen angezeigt; die Mützenschnur verweist auf einen Offizier. Der Ärmelstreif identifiziert das Osloer 'Viken' Regiment. **B2** Zahlreiche deutsche Merkmale lassen sich bei dieser einzigen in Kasernen stationierten Einheit der BDV finden, die aus Russland-Veteranen der SS bestand. **B3** Die Armbinde war natürlich das einzige Abzeichen militärischer Ordnung bei dieser Untergrundeinheit, allerdings erst 1945.

C1 Die frühe Uniform unterschied sich kaum von der der Allgemeinen SS, abgesehen von den Landesabzeichen auf Mütze, Kragen und Ärmel. Der Armstreif identifiziert die Kompanie, in diesem Fall die Reiterkompanie. **C2** Die praktischere Militäruniform, die auf der dänischen Armeebekleidung von 1923 beruht. Man beachte die eigenartigen Kragen und Schulterabzeichen im Gegensatz zur schwarzen Uniform. **C3** Zur Zeit der Befreiung wurden dänische Armeegegenstände von den Widerstandskämpfern offen getragen.

D1 Die Uniform dieses Hauptmanns ist weitgehend identisch mit der seines deutschen Gegenübers, abgesehen vom schwarzen hemd, den Armabzeichen, dem oberen Mützenabzeichen und dem Kragenabzeichen mit der Regimentsnummer. Alle holländischen Einheiten trugen den einfachen Ärmelstreif. **D2** WA-Uniform im SS-Stil mit roten Kragenabzeichen und je nach Rang (hier ein Major) unterschiedlicher Farbe des Schnurbesatzes auf der Mütze. Das Dreiecksabzeichen gehört zum NSB. **D3** Nach einem der wenigen erhaltenen Fotos von dieser Einheit: Das Granatenabzeichen erinnert an die Gemeindepolizei, aus der die Mitglieder dieser Einheit stammten.

E1 Wie die holländischen Kollaborateure benutzte auch die Schwarze Brigade die schwarzen Uniformen und Wolfshakenruen als Abzeichen. Ursprünglich hatten die grünen Kragenabzeichen die Form der italienischen 'Flammen', später wurden sie durch SS-ähnliche Abzeichen ersetzt. **E2** Man beachte die Bataillonsnummer auf Brust und Mütze, Rangabzeichen auf Schulterstreifen und einfache Kragenabzeichen für alle Ränge; deutsche *Tresse* für Kragen und Schulterstreifen. Die entsprechende *Garde Wallonne* trug die gleiche Uniform aber mit rotem Schnurbesatz. **E3** Die von der Luftwaffe ausgehobene und ausgerüstete Einheit hatte WA, Luftwaffe und SS Stile in der letzten Ausführung der Uniform.

F1 Man beachte das Fehlen der Schulterstreifen und Rangabzeichen sowie die von diesen Teilzeit-Milizmännern getragenen Zivilhemden; dazu eine Mischung aus französischen und deutschen Verzierungen—er ist wahrscheinlich ein ehemaliger LVF-Veteran. **F2** Eine von vielen kleinen französischen faschistischen Milizen, die meist blaue Hemden trugen. **F3** Ein *maquisard* von 1944, in Begleitung der landenden Alliierten bei schweren Gefechten.

G1 Diese zum Volkssturm gehörenden Tiroler Bataillone trugen grüne Kragenabzeichen, da sie von der Polizei ausgehoben wurden. Man beachte das Armabzeichen und die fehlenden Schulterstreifen. **G2** Die einzige Partisanengruppe mit kompletter Uniform; man beachte die *Edelweiss*-Kragenabzeichen und die CVL-ähnlichen Rangabzeichen. **G3** Einer der verbreitetsten unter den verschiedenen Kragenabzeichen, die von den GNR-Männern getragen wurden; die kragenlose Jacke und die weiten Hosen waren bei den RSI Einheiten sehr beliebt. Barrette und Alpenhüte waren die Alternativen für diese Feldmütze.

H1 Armee-ähnliche Uniform und Marine-ähnliche Rangabzeichen; die Kragenabzeichen ähneln denen der Marineinfanteristen, und die Ärmelabzeichen beruhen auf denen der alten Motor-Torpedobootflotilla des Fürsten Borghese. **H2** Es gibt nur wenige Unterschiede zur früheren Kgl. Armee-Uniform, abgesehen von der fehlenden Krone in allen Abzeichen und dem Schwert/Kranz-Motiv auf dem Kragen sowie dem fehlenden Rangabzeichen auf den Manschetten. **H3** Brigadeabzeichen auf der linken Brustseite; der Rang wird durch die runden Schnurabzeichen angegeben.